Crime Scene Psychic:
Evidence of the Afterlife

Angela McGhee

All rights reserved. No part of this book may be reproduced by any mechanical, photographic or electronic process, or in the form of a phonographic recording; nor may it be stored in a retrieval system, transmitted or otherwise be copied for public or private use, other than for 'fair use' as brief quotations embodied in articles and reviews, without prior written permission of the publisher.

The author of this book does not dispense medical advice or prescribe the use of any technique as a form of treatment for physical or medical problems without the advice of a physician, either directly or indirectly. The intent of the author is only to offer information of a general nature to help you in your quest for emotional and spiritual wellbeing. In the event you use any of the information in this book for yourself, which is your constitutional right, the author and the publisher assume no responsibility for your actions.

ISBN 978-1-54069-263-4

Photo credits:
page 36 : Family of Danny Fielder
page 60: Family of Leah Schafer-Desormeau
page 81: Family of Alpha Sey
page 82: Family of Alan Heyden
page 121: Family of Josh Heelas
page 152:Family of Cian McBrine
page 182: Family of Martin Green
page 188: Family of Buster Knight
page 194: Family of Barry Latta
page 206: Family of Keilyn Kerr
page 263: Family of Bailey Wootten

© Angela McGhee, 2017

DEDICATION

To my mother and my children

ACKNOWLEDGMENTS

It is with heartfelt gratitude to all those families involved in the book and those who sealed their 'loved ones' communication with a photograph.

FOREWARD

Angela McGhee is a highly respected Psychic Medium whose 'visions' have been publicly acclaimed by Chief Police Officers of the UK. Her 'visions' have become an investigative tool that can bring clues or new evidence to lines of enquiries. Angela has been brought into unsolved 'cold' cases when all traditional methods have been exhausted. Nothing really warrants the fact that she is called the 'Psychic Detective' other than the results her mind produces in such circumstances. The 'visions' produced have played a key part in the gathering of evidence. Details of such events may otherwise been left unnoticed and as for the perpetrators of such crimes, amazingly, she has been able to build a detailed profile of such individuals in question, noting such details as life story events and personality traits. Angela does not solve crimes as such, the Police do... Her 'Gifts are considered a 'key tool' in the proceedings to gather clues, evidence and confirmation of lines of enquiries to say the least.

Here she chronicles, details of soul-wrenching accounts of her involvement in such cases and more importantly the life experiences which led her to the work she does today.

Those crucial experiences that have helped to mold a unique pathway, to developing and understanding the 'Psychic' Gifts 'which she was blessed to be born with. Her work is a real eye-opener for the most sceptical of people and for those who are seeking the knowledge of the Afterlife and its power to seek justice, help and understanding. This 'evidential' document undoubtedly, makes Angela McGhee one of the world's leading 'Psychic Detectives'.

Angela is renowned for her spine- chilling appearance in the worldwide Classic U.S .TV series 'Psychic Investigators'. She is also a successful Author, Columnist and has guested on many programmes in the Media worldwide.

She has successfully toured the UK and Europe, presenting her unique 'Psychic Detective' workshops, talks. Seminar and ground- breaking demonstrations of Mediumship.

Jules McCarthy BBC Journalist

www.angelamcghee.com

A poem dedicated to Angela McGhee...

How can you know what I wanted to hear,
to bring my loved one so close and so near.,
You take me back to a moment in time
convey the unspoken set down in rhyme.,
You touch my spirit, enfold my heart,
for a moment in time we are not apart.
You transcend and touch my loved one's soul,
communicate with heaven given your role
And show me your mind in that infinite space,
how love is transposed to that special place.
A union of minds for just you and I,
energized channeling just passing by.
Proof that my son is watching over me
in a spiritual place where he truly is free,
Giving me strength in life to move on,
knowing my child has not really gone.

Written by Annie Stokes.

(A mother, whose heart was 'inspired' to write this poem, who in turn has touched my soul.)

CONTENTS

1. Police Profiler.............4

2. No Distance................22

3. Three Amigos...............30

4. Sonny.........................38

5. The Afterlife Show......47

6. Beverly's Angel...........56

7. Murder on Air.............62

8. Twelve little Angels...70

9. Job Description...........87

10. Days Off....................99

11. Josh.........................115

12. Hard Day's Night.......124

13. Internationale.......132

14. Proud Feather..........139

15. The Fairy Godmother..145

16. Call of Duty...............156

17. The little Pebble...................159

18. Heavens Pension 165

19. Spirit Union..........................171

20. Seeking Justice....................177

21. Martin..................................179

22. Buster.................................183

24. Baz II 189

25. Keilyn.................................197

26. Missing..............................208

27. Maddie...............................220

28. Micheal..............................235

29. Death..................................242

30. Gifts of the Soul................247

POLICE PROFILER

It was no coincidence that during my daily travels; the subject of two missing boys kept cropping up in conversations. It was during separate private sittings, and all in a short space of time. I was asked by my clients whether I had ever received any information about the two boys. The boys had gone missing over ten years ago, and although I didn't live far from the location, I was baffled as to why I couldn't remember seeing any media coverage at the time.

I soon worked out the reason. The timing of the incident coincided with a trauma in my personal life, which was when my eldest son was in hospital for nearly a year recuperating from illness.

I was 'beside myself', so much so that I was almost oblivious to all news and events. My son's welfare was the only focus during this long period.

The recent subject of the missing boys in conversations, continued to draw my attention but didn't make an impact on my 'psyche' until one Easter Sunday afternoon in April, whilst I was watching television.

In a flash, once again, my thoughts were interrupted by a 'vision'. I could see two boys going through a gate, an entrance to a patch of woodland; there was something about the gate that looked unusual. I could see the gate's access which led to a path, where there was a stretch of water to the left, trees to the right and within a short distance along the path, one could see the brow of a small hill.

I was alarmed when I realized my 'vision' was relating to the two boys in question. I sensed that these woods were close by to where they had once lived.

At this point I felt I couldn't do anything about it or contact anyone, as the clients who had asked me about it, had no real connection with the boys or their families.

Realizing this, I felt helpless but nevertheless I did feel inclined to go to the area myself and have a look around. But it was my son who convinced me otherwise that day, saying that I would look rather suspicious, and he reminded me tat woodlands were not the safest of places either.

It took some time to get over those unsettled feelings attached to the 'visions', but I came to the resolution that maybe in future a further, a more substantial connection would be made, as in my 'usual' cases of spirit communication as I know that the spirit world does not use that amount of energy communicating for very little purpose or reason, so it was a case of biding my time and spirits' time, for the right moment for the greater picture to unfold.

I attempted to put these 'visions' to the back of my mind, only to find they would occasionally resurface in the weeks that followed, as they filtered and etched their way into my conscious mind. The 'visions' came into my dream state too. I was convinced something more would happen but didn't know quite when.

It was over six months later in November, that I had a telephone call from a lady named Pauline, who sounded somewhat 'mysterious' at first. She said she had read one of my books and wanted to introduce me to a retired Detective Chief Inspector, whose role had actually been a Head in Crime Intelligence .His request was to take me to locations relating to a particular case, which was in the process of being reopened due to new evidence he had personally discovered.

It related to the case of the two missing boys, but I was told there were other cases that he wanted me to 'help' with too.

She gave little information, other than the fact the

Detective was named Bob and that he would be phoning me to make arrangements for us to meet up.

I could not hold back any longer. I shared with her, what I had already 'received'. I was so right to think I would have a connection, and things were about to take a platform.

It was 9am on a cold November morning. I drove my car onto a Superstore car park, where I was met by Bob. He appeared to be quite a friendly character, but I sensed an underlying stern edge of authority about him. He suggested we travel in his car. He asked me to be prepared for a long day ahead, as there were several locations he wanted to take me to. I then told him of the 'vision' I had way back in April. I emphasized that the gate I had 'seen' was very unusual.

"I think I know where that is. We will go there a bit later but there's somewhere I want to take you first." he said.

We drove a few miles passing a number of housing estates, where all of the houses looked very similar. It was like we were going round in circles. It was a part of the city I was not familiar with. It was like a maze.

As we drove along, Bob filled me in on what he hoped to achieve that day, if anything at all. He seemed very cautious of what information he divulged to me and told me that, if there was anywhere in particular I'd like to be taken to, that I should not hesitate to ask. He tended to talk a lot but at the same time being careful not to give me any information or leading suggestions. His professional jargon and intellect was none the less intriguing.

In my mind I was saying a quick prayer or two as we travelled along. It would be a lie to say that I didn't feel anxious. It was just the seriousness of it all that gave it an edge. I was hoping that my anxieties would not put a block up to the 'spirit world's' communication.

Suddenly, Bob pulled the car up into the side of a busy road, in the middle of a housing estate.

"Now then Angela, do you pick up on anything around here?"

I glanced around looking at a dozen houses or more in front of me, just hoping and praying. The houses were all very similar.

I then blurted out an answer, as usual, being instrumented by my Guides and helpers.

"I... I... I want to go the cul-de-sac that we have just passed back there..." I said, a little nervously, as I twisted my body around to point at the houses behind me.

"Go and have a look then!" Bob said encouragingly.

I got out of the car and walked up the cul-de-sac. I stopped and stared at the second house along. For a few seconds I caught a glimpse of a disturbing 'vision'. It seemed to confuse me as it didn't marry up to what I already knew of the missing boys, but all the same I knew I had to tell Bob of my findings. I was starting to feel very detached as I sensed my Guides were accompanying me.

There was an element of surprise and a realisation on Bob's face when I told him, that when I glanced over at the second house along in the cul-de-sac, I had had a 'vision' of a boy that I knew had been found hanging on the stairwell.

Before Bob could answer me, I told him I felt it had happened in the 1980s. I looked at Bob for some reassurance But it was as if my tongue got carried away and was obviously being totally 'instrumented' as I added

: "It has something to do with a lodger in the house."

"Yes! You're exactly right Angela, I can explain a little now," he said. There was a boy found in that house, hanging on the stairwell in 1981, but back then it was labelled as a suicide. We think otherwise now and have a prime suspect, who apparently was the lodger in that house at the time."

Something else began to build up in my mind. It's as if 'those in spirit' had started to build a 'Profile' of the lodger. I began to 'sense' even more about him as my thoughts began to flow. The Spirit World was beginning to match the profile known to Bob. I continued to tell Bob of what I was receiving.

"This man drove a small white van, and he had something to do with gardening. He was a general handy-man type and I feel he'd had a connection with the Navy at one point in his life."

Bob nodded with his eyebrows raised, gesturing, encouraging me to say more.

"There's a pub called The Trooper or The Soldier, something to do with the military, this has a connection to him too. Although the culprit was a loner, he could be a quite an articulate man but seemed very popular with his 'circle' of friends."

I then had another 'vision' and saw what appeared to be another cul-de-sac. This one seemed to have some sort of pig farm situated at the end. I told Bob this, and as I looked at Bob for confirmation, I felt the flow of 'energy' diminishing slightly.

"Well Angela, I can tell you that this man did drive a small white van, he seemed to be a 'jack of all trades'. He had quite a few manual outdoor jobs in fact. And the pub that you mentioned is actually called 'The Trooper', which is situated not far from the cul-de-sac where he once lodged. In fact he used to be the Pub's quiz-master there. He seemed to be a very popular character and as for the pig farm you mentioned, I think I'll take you there now. This was one of the places where he did some work too."

In my mind, I thanked God for all that I received.

"I thought I was asked here, in connection with two boys?" I said.

"The prime suspect to do with the boy on the stairwell is the same prime suspect in the missing boy's case too." Bob explained. It all made perfect sense.

We drove to the pig farm. I didn't sense much there, other than the fact it confirmed the whereabouts and its significance to the suspect. Bob suggested that we go to the place I described in my very first 'vision', the one with the unusual gate. He said I would find it very interesting.

We meandered through the housing estates and through some greenbelt land. We turned into a country road, which had thickets of trees aligning each side. Bob stopped the car and there was the gate, the patch of water, the woodland, and the brow of a hill beyond.

"This type of gate was actually called a 'kissing gate'." Bob informed me. That was something new I learned and it seemed it wasn't going to be the only thing that I learned that day.

"Yes! Yes! Bob, this is it. This is what I 'saw'. This is where two boys took me in my mind, as I seem to follow them into these woods" I said.

Bob seemed engrossed in the findings and went over my visions linking them to the facts. He began to build upon the information I had already given him. He was fascinating to listen to, as he started to talk about the classic patterns of behavior and the psychological traits of certain offenders, who commit such horrific crimes. He was building a 'Profile' and it was fascinating to listen to. He taught me what to look for. I learnt about some aspects of what the police call 'tracking', particularly in wooded areas, and the ways in which culprits try to disguise and hide things. He explained how nature reacts and gives tell-tale signs to such intrusions. Bob described how such culprits will only walk a certain distance to bury their evidence and how quite commonly, they bury it on the edge of woodland. Woodlands seemed to be a popular place to hide the evidence of such particular crimes. Apparently once the ground has been dug for any disposal, the culprit will often dig round in a circle, rather than a trough-like shape, so that when the ground concaves and settles, it will look more natural.

It all sounded very clever and devious, but obviously there is a cunning logic behind their evil actions. All this profiling was an eye opener. It upset me to hear of their sickening evil ways.

I was most surprised when I learnt about 'search procedures' too. When open land searches are done under Police operations, we imagine them using some kind of high tech ground-trawling radar equipment. I was informed that forces are actually only equipped and reliable on man power, numbers of men who themselves are only equipped with a spear shaped metal rod and a sniffer dog. The technique is to pierce the ground and show the 'sniffer' dog, in the hope of positive 'reaction'.

It's as basic as that. I was shocked as the procedures seemed very primitive to me, especially in this age of new technology that we live in. I can understand why people like me are called in for 'help'. Nevertheless, to experiment with the spirit world is just another alternative way to help and gain answers or shall I say confirm lines of enquiries as the case maybe. Listening to Bob was certainly an 'education' for me.

Bob then pointed to the 'brow' of a hill.

"Angela, do you see the little hill you described? It is in fact a man-made grassy mound. It is the result of a land clearance, which made way for a golfing range. This golfing range is situated just behind the hill and that is where our prime suspect was once employed. He was the caretaker of the Range. And he lived in a caravan on the site, which seems close enough to the woods to benefit him."

I had no doubt in my mind that this area was of great significance to the disappearance of the two missing boys.

Time seemed to fly by that day. It seemed like I'd spent the best part of the day in 'three worlds', this world, that of spirit but also Bob's world. Each world being, equally truly fascinating and humbling.

I have nothing but admiration for people like Bob for what they have to deal with on almost a daily basis, as they endure such horrors in their working lives. I am fortunate I only get a small 'glimpse' of their world, enough to be valuable but not self soul destroying.

In hindsight, I think Bob had planned an agenda for the

day, taking me to places, in a specific order so he could to build a clearer picture to the known facts. And maybe the place for the 'beginning' was a good start and obviously had very good reason.

He then took me to a number of parks, where again I did not sense anything as relevant as before, other than a significant connection with the prime suspect.

It was getting late in the afternoon, and dusk was about to embark. It was then I realised several hours had passed. I thought Bob was about to 'call it a day,' when he threw in one last request. It was to be our final location, so he reassured me. He could see I was beginning to look physically tired, not to mention hungry, but the severity of the hours that passed, connected to spirit, seemed to numb my physical needs.

At this point I was beginning to doubt the 'force' of my psychic abilities. I felt uncertain as to whether they would 'work' when I had started to feel so drained, added to the fact, that for the last hour or so I hadn't 'received' as clearly as before. I obliged all the same but with more hope this time. I continued to pray under my breath.

Again, we arrived at another stretch of woods, which appeared much denser, as there were a lot more trees this time. We parked up in a lay-by opposite.

"Come on Angela..." Bob said as if he was straining the last bit of my 'energy'.

This was to be our last 'hurdle' of the day, and my God I certainly wasn't prepared or conditioned for what I was about to 'see'.

As we entered the woods, I noticed a block of concrete lying on the ground. I felt 'drawn to it' and I mentioned what I felt to Bob. He told me it had some significance to where he was taking me.

As we scrambled through the long woodland growth. It seemed to get darker with every step and I found myself surrounded by literally hundreds of trees. Dusk was beginning to settle. I glanced around intensely and noticed the 'significant sign'. One particular tree had a similar concrete block, which seemed to have been thrown across its roots. The impact of what I saw next was totally devastating. I had a 'vision'. There was a young man hanging from the bough of the tree. It took my breath away.

Bob seemed to be meandering in the trees, some distance away from me.

"Bob! Bob!" I shouted, and beckoned him to come quickly. He obviously kept his distance, as not to give me any geographical clues.

"There's a young man there!" I said pointing up at the tree. Bob was getting used to my ways by now. I looked away from the 'vision' as quick as I could as it was so, so vivid. It may have been the backdrop of the day's sunlight fading, that the 'vision' was illuminated with even more energy.

Bob knew exactly what I meant, as he asked.

"You can see a young man…" Bob said calmly, questioning me.

This questioning was totally unexpected but in hindsight it was for obvious reasons. Bob seemed to put his 'interrogation hat' on.

"Right then Angela, what can you tell me, can you tell me what colour, the rope is?"

It was the first time that a 'vision' had been demanded on 'request'. But sure enough, I 'saw' it again. I told Bob the boy's name was Mark and that the rope was blue and that it had two knots in it and also there was something which looked like some kind of ring attached to it.

Bob nodded with a knowing look on his face.

"I have a photo of that rope in the car… the fact that you mentioned the knots, they are something very significant…" he informed me.

Bob must have thought he could question the spirit world, and instantly get a string of answers. And so you can but I thought my 'energy' levels would fail me. His questions were being 'listened' to, so it seemed.

I had never been placed in such a 'pressured' position before. Bob continued his interrogation of me and the spirit world.

"Now then, Angela. Could you tell me what the boy is wearing?"

I composed myself and held myself together. I took a quick glimpse of the tree and the 'vision' and I said very quickly, "He's wearing a T-shirt and jeans."

Just then, I had another vision of the same place. This time there was a man, standing alongside the tree, winching up the boy's body. I began to realise the horror of it all.

Aghast, I said, "There's a man pulling on the rope, who is standing alongside the tree winching up the boy's body..."

The reality of my 'vision' had great impact as the truth hit me. "My God... this boy was murdered... and then strung up!"

Tears started to fill my eyes. I was finding it very difficult to speak.

"What does the man look like Angela?" Bob asked. I knew I had no choice but to look again.

"He's wearing khaki coloured clothes and a hand knitted woolly hat," I described his hat, "it's something like Benny out of *Crossroads* wore." I said comparing it to a TV soap character, from an era, that I knew Bob would be familiar with.

"I actually have a photograph of 'our man' in question wearing that hat." Bob replied.

I was beginning to feel depletion in the 'energy' and as it took mine with it. "That's it. There is no more I can give." I said to Bob.

My Helpers and Guides were dispersing.

"Good girl." Bob said, as if it were a final pat on the back. He could see and feel the impact it was having on me.

I sensed Bob was a sensitive man deep down. And it was obvious by his reactions that he had a deep understanding of Mediumship. After all he was a highly intelligent, well-read man. I had no doubt that the subject of 'my kind' of findings, had been read somewhere too and he had grasped a good understanding. He wouldn't be the first officer to tell me that he worked with his 'gut' feeling either.

Bob began to make a summary of the day's events. "You know what Angela, I must tell you that I had Doris Stokes (a renowned medium, who is now deceased,) involved in this case back in the 1980s and you are telling me the same as she did, if not more. I want to thank you, so much for the time you've given me today. The things you've said have been a real eye opener, fascinating and a real help. It takes someone really special to do what you've done. You have been remarkable and I can't thank you enough." he said.

He went onto describe how Doris Stokes became involved in the case. He said he had accompanied his wife, to one of her Theatre shows in London. Doris relayed a 'message' to Bob from a boy call Mark, who she described, had passed in such circumstances , up here in the Midlands. Bob said he had been totally intrigued by her,as he was working on that case at that said time. She became involved after Bob gained a meeting with her in her London home, Bob said she was a very friendly down to earth lady. She introduced me to her son Terry. He had some kind of Learning difficulties but that did not hinder him working As he drove for a living. We had another connection funnily enough, when Terry phoned one day to say that his mother had died and that he had been to her Bank account and discovered it was empty. He had turned to me for help. I instigated the Fraud investigation, apparently her Agent had helped himself to her life savings, more so, Terry's inheritance. She did die penniless, as the Media reported. But through fraud.

Again, what I found strange, was that one evening ,during work, I went to see a body in the morgue , whereas, back in those days Birmingham had one central Morgue. It was when I closing a draw on a body, I noticed the name on the draw alongside it. It was labeled 'Terry Stokes'. My instinct told me to open the drawer and there was Terry , Doris's son, who had died in motorway crash, up here in the Midlands.

I 'knew' Bob 'knew,' there was so much more to this 'psychical' life.

He gave me an appreciative hug and a pat on the back. I thanked my Guides and Helpers over and over again, but nevertheless I was relieved totally, moved and immensely humbled by it all.

What could I say to that? I answered a call of duty that day, not only to the spirit world but to Bob too.

The feeling of presence was immense at times as the 'visions' became so luminous. I had no doubt that Bob's thoughts had drawn Doris Stokes' Spirit also. It was obvious that there was a number of different 'helpers' working with me, which reflected amidst the abundance of energy I felt . Although I thought what I felt at times, that day seemed to be faltering.

It became obvious that those helpers continued to battle through my emotions and psychical tiredness, giving me the unmistakable strength, to enable me to pass on very valuable and correct information and validations.

I eventually arrived home feeling totally exhausted and not without admitting feeling traumatized. It was several weeks before the memory of the horrific 'visions' disappeared to the back of my mind as I found myself having some kind of physical, psychological 'flashbacks'. But it was not until sometime later I felt the job satisfaction you gain from the 'sense of duty' that my work often entails.

I would like to thank and bless all those involved in this incident, some whose true identities I have not disclosed out of privacy and respect.

I would also like to transcend my loving thoughts to Doris Stokes, the pioneering Medium whose work. appears to still continue from the other side.. Bless her.

This particular case was one of the most remarkable cases I have 'worked' on so far, as there have been many cases of such nature, where my Psychic abilities, my gifts, have been utilised to find answers. Such requests have come from many Police Detectives, Journalists and victims' families, who are seeking answers to life's most devastating and painful problems.

And it seems that it is those 'Souls of the Spirit World' who have passed in such circumstances, those who have left this earthly plane in such dramatic ways. Their spirit seems to 'seek me out'.

I am a 'down to earth' Woman, a Mother and an ex-Social Worker, born with a Gift, which I reluctantly had to discover, nurture and gain an understanding of life's true purpose, along a journey of self-discovery albeit touched by one's own grief, trauma and tragedy.

The Spirit Communication used in this case expressed a 'pinnacle' of my Gift's abilities. The pinnacle reached was another 'crescendo' to every 'Spiritual' experience that had gone before me. It was only during the process of time, my own self-discovery was sketched by some of the following experiences

NO DISTANCE

Delivering the service of Mediumship has involved an immense amount of travel over the years, locally, nationally, and even globally. Travel, whether in person, by voice or by written word.

The realms of spirit hold no boundaries once we discover we are an instrument. We are all open to attune ourselves to the power of spirit, God's spirit and the spiritual realms. It is a 'force' which is present and moves mysteriously within our physical world.

Although it all seems a mystery, the first step to unravelling that mystery is a 'belief'. All you have to do is have a belief in God and when you 'believe' it, then you will 'receive' the 'keys' to the knowledge of the 'unseen world'. I was fortunate enough to be given that 'key' at birth. A key, a 'gift' of communication.

There was a time in my life when I started to reach even more people with my wisdom. I used to be invited to visit people in their homes, like a doctor on call, dishing out my daily doses of healing words, giving comfort to those who needed my help the most.

I found it quite apt when years after; BBC journalist Jules McCarthy made a summary of my work after witnessing one of my theatre shows.

She complimented me by stating that 'Angela McGhee should be available on Prescription'. It was quite apt, I thought, after all my intention is to make people feel so much better, after giving them a 'dose' of 'heavenly' communication.

Sometimes, the 'tools' within life's lessons that we gain today, become the 'tools' we need in the future.

It was when our wider computerized era began, that the following incidences made me realize, that the spirit world was preparing me for work in a different way, at a higher level and at a longer distance. I recall one afternoon when I received a telephone call from a man who spoke in broken English with an unfamiliar accent.

"Hello, is that Angela McGhee? My name is Karim Yaberi. I am phoning you from Iran," he said. "I want you to talk to spirit. I want you to come to Iran. Money is nothing... I make you welcome. Please, if you can be so kind, as I am kissing your hand many times, Miss Angela." he professed.

At first I thought it was a prank call of some sort. But as I listened to him talk, I eventually sensed the authenticity in his tone. I asked him to repeat himself a couple of times until it actually registered that the call was indeed genuine. I was very surprised about the fact he was calling me from Iran and even more surprised he had heard of me and what I do.

I smiled to myself thinking that I couldn't go to Iran that week as I had Ward End church to serve.

"Where did you get my number?" I asked him, out of curiosity.

"I got it from the S.N.U. register (the Spiritualist National Union) from a website." he replied.

I was intrigued and wanted to find out more. "There must be at least a couple of hundred names on that list. Why did you choose mine?" I asked him.

"Because you have name of an Angel..." he replied.

His trail of thought did make some sense amidst his flattery, but his comment made me smile nonetheless. Could I really communicate spiritually down the telephone line, all the way to Iran, I began to ask myself.

My thoughts were soon dismissed by the voice in my mind coming from my Spirit Guide. As she told me, "The power of God's work is beyond the universe."

My trail of thought was back on track as I remembered

everything I had achieved with spirit communication during national calls across the U.K. Those long distance calls turned out to be quite remarkable.

With this knowledge strong in my mind, I was sure this International request would be no different.

I must admit I still continued to feel a little apprehensive after sensing that it was his father's spirit he wished to receive communication from, which he agreed was the case.

"Yes! Yes! It is my father I want... I want you to manifest his spirit and talk to him." he said bluntly.

I got a clear picture of what he was trying to say in his limited vocabulary, and got the impression by his tone that he thought I could simply wave some kind of a 'magic wand' and manifest his father's spirit in front of me and have a full conversation with him there and then.

I decided to explain to him more detail about Mediumship and how it was not a case of being able to manifest his father's spirit on demand, as his suggestion seemed to indicate.

I informed Karim of some of the profound and subtle ways in which our loved ones can communicate. I told him it was a case of whether his father's spirit or his father's Guides wished to communicate or not as the case may be, so I felt I had to educate him a little on this vast subject.

Feeling a little unsure, I decided the best thing to do was to suggest that he wrote to me, enclosing a photograph of his father. I promised him that I would see what I could sense and feel and hopefully receive communication from his father's spirit.

Two weeks later, I received a letter from him with an enclosed copy of an old passport sized photograph of his father. In the letter Karim suggested that I set up an email. An email was something I was not familiar with at the time, as computer technology was only on the brink of reaching our local libraries and just becoming readily available to us all.

In any case, I visited the local library and asked the kind assistant to help me with this new facility called email. An email seemed like a whole new phenomenon to me, let alone a new form of communication in the world of technology.

With Karim's fathers photograph in hand I placed it in front of me. Leaning it up against the screen of the computer as I began to type my email. I began waiting for my Spirit Guides and those in spirit to help. I began to type, it seemed that my mind and fingers were being influenced.

The first thing I sensed was that Karim had three sons who had links with America and Paris, and that Karim also had a wife who had crossed over. I also sensed there was a baby who had crossed over in pregnancy too.

I began to 'visualize' his father in spirit. I described him as a small, stocky man with a beard, who wore a large ruby ring on his left hand, and that he walked with the help of a cane.

In the letter that Karim had sent he had asked if Spirit would be able to tell him whether his father had made a will or not and if he had, where it could be found. I realized that this was the paramount purpose of his letter.

I began to 'see' papers slotted between pages of a book that looked worn, but clearly was not just an ordinary book. It became clear it was a holy book. In fact, it was the Quran.

As I continued to write the email, I felt I needed to explain again even more detail about the different aspects of my Mediumship and how Spirit worked and communicated with me. So I added an extra paragraph or two.

It was then when I felt that I was coming to end of the communication I 'heard' two names. This took me totally by surprise. One of the names I'd never heard of. These were obviously Iranian names. The two name that were given were Abdoul and Vahid. I knew they connected with Karim in some way. I surprised myself as obviously I couldn't talk Iranian but with confidence and inspiration I mentioned them. This was the last thought from the spirit which ended the email and communication.

I anxiously clicked on the 'send' button and released my first email to the power of technology, spirit and the universe. I had placed my full trust in my Spirit Guides once again.

But it was only by the power of technology that it was not long before I received a reply to my email. I was blown away by Karim's response. He seemed extremely shocked by what I told him. He told me that what had shocked him the most was the two names I had given him; this was the first thing he mentioned. He confirmed the majority of what I had written had rung true but it was the fact that the two names I'd given were his middle names, names that only his father would know.

His email reply began with him asking me, how I could possibly know these names, for they were 'secret identity names'.as he said in his broken English. He explained that it was only his Father who called him these names, no one else.

The power of spirit can work within and beyond the power of technology as it is 'greater than the universe' by what I had already been told by my Guide.

It was such a remarkable experience. I printed off the email to keep and to add to my collection of cherished reminders. All of these mementos are evidence of the spirit world.

I will never forget Karim and his incredible email as they played a significant and poignant part in my spiritual development and understanding. Not to mention it helped me improve my computer skills.

THREE AMIGOS

I recall a spate of new experiences like an escalation, a rise in my heightened awareness. It became apparent that the spirit world was going to show me things that I had not witnessed before. A spiraling spiritual evolution began to take place. It seemed spirit was enacting change within me, to enable people to enact change.

A key stage was when I was contacted by my cousin Maria. She wrote to me to ask for a favour, as she knew I wouldn't mind helping her. She asked me if I would be kind enough to talk to a woman called Kathy who she had given my telephone number to. She told me that Kathy would be calling me, as her son Danny had recently passed over and that she was desperate to talk to a Medium.

Maria explained that Kathy was actually a relative, a distant cousin of ours although I had never heard of her or met her before.

Maria had enclosed a photograph of three people gathered together. It was a photograph of Kathy with two young teenage boys standing alongside her. Maria marked the photo indicating which one of the boys was Danny, Kathy's son. That was all the information Maria gave me, other than the fact that Kathy would be calling me one evening in the near future.

The telephone call came a bit later than I expected one evening. My house was unusually quiet, as the children were not at home at that time. I had been sitting alone, relaxing in meditative thought when the phone rang.

It was Kathy, apologizing for phoning late. The timing and conditions seemed right. It was obvious by the tones in her voice she was desperate to hear something from her beloved son.

I instantly began to connect with her son's spirit. A clear and vivid picture of him materialized in my mind. It wasn't just the reflection of his face, as he appeared in the photograph I had. I could also hear and see him talk.

His communication began with the name of his home town, as I said to her.

"Your Danny is here, Kath. He's okay, I must tell you."

I assured Kathy he looked well and that there was so much love he wanted to send her. I caught on to his first words as more of a connection unfolded.

I told her Danny was talking of Huyton. Coincidentally, Huyton is a suburb of Liverpool where I had once resided for a short time, as a child.

"That's where I'm from, and where Danny was bought up." Kathy replied.

Danny's presence was overwhelming. His presence equaled the power of his youthful energy. His spirit seemed to entwine with mine as he used my 'vessel' to communicate. It seemed I was in a semi-trance state. I became aware that Danny was showing me through his own eyes, what he could see in this life. His spirit guided me on a 'guided tour', around his home, introducing me to his family that evening.

I was feeling extremely detached and elevated from where I was sitting. At the same time his spirit seemed so close within mine.

My mind's eye began to scan what Danny could see. A panoramic view seemed to reel before me, as I told Kathy I could see an Entry house. I sensed Danny was showing me his home so effectively. Kathy then confirmed she did in fact live in an 'Entry' house.

I was taken by his spirit, up the side of the house. I began to tell Kathy what I could 'see' or rather the case of what I was being shown. Each step and movement was confirmed by Kathy who seemed to show very little reaction in the tones in her voice. On reflection I suppose she was shocked by what was happening and found it almost unbelievable. I was so much in awe, as I always am in awe of spirit when I work but these experiences had me enraptured. It continued...

Danny's spirit then trailed my mind into a backyard where I could see bicycle parts scattered around. I felt that these had lain untouched for months, since his passing. I strongly sensed his love of bikes too.

Kathy informed me then, that this was just so and that Danny had died as a result of a bike accident.

With Danny's spirit entwined with mine, I was taken on a journey around his home. I was a witness to something that I had not seen before. It was as if I was seeing things through Danny's eyes, exactly what his spirit could see. I was 'shown' into the living room.

I told Kathy that Danny was showing me a school photograph of himself and his sister that hung on a wall, above the sofa. I told Kathy that I knew Danny had sister, and consequently a brother too.

"Yes, yes..." Kathy replied nervously.

It was then in my accompanied vision, I was taken up the stairs almost in 'flight'. Danny was eager to show me around. I was shown his bedroom, where he and his brother had shared bunk beds.

I spoke to Kathy about his brother and the difference between them. His brother's love of football equaled Danny's passion for bikes. These hobbies made up the difference between them. Their differences were expressed by the pictures they each had hung in their allocated wall spaces above their beds, which I could 'see'.

All the time during Danny's altered communication; I had been holding the photograph that my cousin Maria had sent me.

"The other boy that stands alongside Danny in the photograp, is in spirit too, so Danny tells me…" I said, as I glanced down at it.

"Yes he is, he too was killed in a bike accident." came the sad reply.

The vibration of Danny's spirit was separating from mine as I could sense him leaving. Then I saw Danny standing in front of me in a 'vision'. He had a young boy of a similar age, standing alongside him. He was different to the boy in the photograph that I was still holding in my hand. I heard Danny shout from a distance, "I'm with Colin."

"Kathy, I don't 'see' Danny with the boy in this photograph, he's with someone else here…" I told her he had told me.'He was with someone named Colin'.

At this moment, Kathy screamed to whoever was with her listening in to the telephone conversation.

"He's with Colin…. he's with Colin!" she shouted, as she began to cry.

Kathy seemed to gain great comfort knowing that he was now with Colin. She explained that Colin was his best friend, who had also recently passed over. Kathy then seemed lost for words as she was comforted by her son's communication.

As she continued to cry, my wonderful experience with Danny came to an end. I said my goodbyes to Kathy and I thanked Danny for the journey, we had shared and the new phenomena he had shown me. He certainly is one young man's spirit I will never forget.

Thank you, Danny.

Danny Fielder

SONNY

A beautiful young Asian girl named Pritti, greeted me with a beaming smile, as she answered the door to her home in Wolverhampton. She had arranged for a sitting and had not given me any indication of who she had wished to receive communication from, as usually is the case. It wasn't until moments later that it became clear who she had longed for.

I noticed a number of photographs of different family members hanging on the living room wall. I felt drawn to take notice of her wedding photograph which hung amongst the display. She looked beautiful draped in a red and gold wedding dress standing beside her new husband, who incidentally was a handsome young man. They were both wearing garlands of flowers.

It was then I saw what appeared to be a young man's spirit manifesting beside her in a vision, and the outline of his body began to materialize. It became clear it was her husband who was standing there, as she sat down. I sensed he not been long in the spirit world.

I told Pritti that there was a young man in spirit that draws close to her. I told her it was her husband and that he had a nickname that seemed to have a very westernized sound to it.

"It sounds like sunny, is that correct?" I asked quizzically.

"That's his nickname, spelt Sonny with an O," Pritti said in a surprised tone. "His real name is Sanjay, but only close members of his family would call him that. He was known by most as Sonny." she explained.

I sensed he passed over with a cancer related condition. Pritti confirmed this too.

I became even more aware of Sanjay's spirit and I could see he was holding his throat, indicating a health problem in that area.

"His problem started here," I said holding my own throat, "and I believe it was very quick, within a matter of weeks, so I am being told."

Pritti looked at me pensively as she positioned herself on the edge of the chair. She began to look intrigued.

"He died within six weeks. She said almost robotically. She seemed to show very little emotion at that point.

"Please tell me more… is he with me now?" she asked as her eyes began to fill with tears.

"Yes, of course." I said, as I reassured her that this knowledge I have of him would not be possible without his spirit.

Again I started to feel elevated and extremely distant. I became 'aware' that I was looking down from a height. I was having an aerial view above a hospital room.

It became apparent that Sanjay was showing me what he could see as his spirit left his physical body. I did not want to alarm her in any way by describing the sensation I was feeling or explain my understanding of the process. It was clearly different to most communications but very profound and powerful. Again another Spirit was showing me what they could see through their eyes, but this time as they took their last breath and rose to up above.

I continued to look down on the hospital room, which was filled with a dozen people or more.

I began to question my understanding of hospital regulations, with that amount of people in one room. It became clear these people were surrounding Sanjay. I could clearly see him as he lay on his bed with wires and tubes coming out of his body.

Someone in the crowd that stood around his bed, picked up a little boy and laid the boy on Sanjay's chest. Sanjay made a lifeless effort in an attempt to embrace him for the very last time, just seconds before his final breath.

I described the scene I had witnessed to Pritti. Her

reaction was to cry for a while. It was a powerful set of memories to handle all at once.

"That's exactly what happened. There were fifteen of us around him in the hospital and it was his little boy who he held as he died."

(I knew this way of working was now to become another aspect of my future communications.)

The next thing that Sanjay was showing me was the view outside his home. It was the day of his funeral. It is not unusual for the spirits of loved ones to attend their own funerals, as they are often warmed and touched by the gestures their loved ones have made in their memory. Sanjay seemed overwhelmed on the day of his funeral. I stood up and looked out of the window.

I told her I could see a large blanket of multi coloured flowers on the ground and crowds of people. The crowd was so big in fact, there were police escorts at either end of the street, trying to make an attempt to control the traffic. So many family and friends had wished to pay their last respects. Sanjay was so popular, I told her all of what I could see.. Sanjay began to 'reel' the events of the day in my mind.

I personally had never witnessed a traditional Hindu funeral before but I was witnessing one now, set before my eyes with the help of Sanjay's spirit. Pritti confirmed everything I 'saw'.

Sanjay was 'saying' something about a song.

"There is something about a song that was played." I said.

It seemed I was being contradicted by my own thoughts as I told myself out loud "But they don't play music at Hindu funerals."

Then Pritti explained that I was right to think that. She told me that she had broken Hindu tradition by insisting on playing a song at the funeral. A song that was special to them both. Pritti was still in tears when she recalled that there was a song which was his favorite, and although he didn't have the greatest singing voice, he would often attempt to 'sing' it.

"You're so right. We don't play music at our funerals but we did that day. Is he not telling you what song it was?" she asked.

"I can only give you what I receive, as any good medium will do." I explained.

But suddenly, just as I thought communication was fading, I could hear a song being played in my mind, loud and clear. I almost squealed with delight at the sounds being played in my 'inner' ear.

"It's *I believe I can fly!*" I told her, a song by the R&B artist R. Kelly. That was the song and I told her so, without any doubt in my mind.

Pritti almost squealed with a mixture of surprise and deep emotion. I felt so relieved that she had now got that specific piece of evidence that she had hoped for all along. She knew without an ounce of doubt that her beloved Sanjay was communicating. He went on to tell her that he loved her and that he had been with his little boy, watching him play on the climbing frame in the garden.

"My goodness, my little boy often says he sees daddy in the garden. You're amazing!" Pritti sobbed.

"No, your 'Sonny' is amazing for showing me all this. Bless him." I said, realising without his 'high vibration' of love, it would not be possible.

It is the love we feel within grief that is the key that opens us up to our faith, no matter which denomination we belong to.

Examining these experiences of spirit communication, they were not unlike what is described as 'astral travel' or but coupled with a loved one's spirit and set with an additional reel of total 'visionary' moments.

Scientifically speaking, the related description of this aspect is often called 'Remote Viewing'. I may be a 'Remote viewer' but I consider this to be simply another label placed on my 'gift', a label I acquired some years later.

It was when I was approached by a journalist named Danny Penman, a journalist for the Daily Mail who was doing research for an article into the subject of 'Remote

Viewing'.

He had read and heard about my experiences which had been witnessed on a recent American radio show, where I delivered 'messages' to callers each week via satellite to Los Angeles from my home here in England. Some of those messages have been coupled with my visions, the so-called 'Remote viewing'.

THE AFTERLIFE SHOW

The ability of my gift has been tested over and over again. This time, conditions were set with just a connection with spirit and a person's voice, a caller on live radio.

The spirit world and I would be given yet another test but on a different platform. The recordings I did were for live radio, on *The Afterlife Show*, which was based in Los Angeles and hosted by another impressionable Iranian, a DJ whose professional name was Shaun Valentine. The show actually originated and was first aired in Canada when it was known as '*Talking with Angels*'. After being renamed it was aired for the first time in the U.S.A. in, the City of Angels, Los Angeles, which was yet another synchronicity in my life connected with Angels and loved ones in spirit.

The Afterlife Show became a part of my life for almost three years, as I recorded regular two hour slots each weekend. It was transmitted across the globe from my home, connected via Internet and aired on Radio Stations in the USA such as Coast 101.3FM Florida, KROO 106.1FM Detroit, and Seattle 95.6FM, to name but a few.

Shaun Valentine had first seen me on TV whilst at his home in Los Angeles, one evening. He had been watching my episode of *Psychic Investigators*, a documentary series about Mediums who have helped Police solve real life murders. He decided to contact me and told me he was so impressed by the power of my spiritual communication in the documentary, that he felt inspired to invite me on his Radio show purely for the intention of an interview about my Psychic Detective work. I happily agreed to do this a few weeks later.

It took place on a Sunday afternoon. I sat at the computer readily waiting with headphones and microphone at the ready. We linked up. Shaun was very warm and welcoming, and the interview seemed to 'fly by'.

Just as I thought the interview was coming to a close, Shaun sprang a surprise on me and asked me whether I would like to speak to a couple of callers. I simply couldn't refuse but I must admit I was nervous as the distance and conditions again were a challenge. The callers were allocated six minutes each, during which they hoped for some sort of communication from their loved ones.

"No pressure, no pressure at all…" I said to myself.

The feeling of pressure rose further when I learned that each of the callers had not only requested communication but wanted communication from a particular relative. It was another case of 'spirit on demand'.

I wasn't used to working that way but I remembered

the previous experience I had with Karim and reminded myself that anything is possible when you believe and trust wholeheartedly in 'spirit'. As the callers were being introduced I said an extra prayer or two.

This was indeed a different way of working. I had always believed that you received communication from the spirit of whoever was ready and able to communicate and that I had no choice in the matter. So I thought, although I have been fortunate through my own experiences over the years, in that ninety-nine per cent of the messages received have been from the particular loved ones, that the recipients were hoping for. Still, I wondered had this all happened by chance? Or did I have the ability to demand spirit?

In the case of the first two callers on The Afterlife Show, they got the evidence of the loved ones they had 'demanded' and hoped for. But God knows what your prayers (requests) are, before you've even asked, so I believe.

Nevertheless, as a Medium you always need to leave room for an element of surprise, as unexpected loved ones often communicate instead.

Taking this into consideration, Shaun would remind callers of this by referring to a quote from a well-known film.

"Communication from our loved ones is like a box of chocolates, you never know what you're gonna get".

Agreeing to put myself in the 'hot seat' that day, I had relayed my first of many demanding messages to callers of a global network via satellite to Los Angeles and several other States.

After the show Shaun thanked me. He seemed very pleased, leaving an open invitation to another show in the near future. Again, I gladly accepted.

It was a few weeks later that I was scheduled to do a second show. This time it was planned that I would receive more callers, as well as talk about different aspects on the subject of Spirituality.

In the intro to the show, Shaun, sheepishly told me he had something to tell me.

"America lurrves you honey!" He said in his American drawl.

I literally giggled at the thought, but with 'tongue in cheek' I quickly quipped back, "Can I have that in writing from the President, please?"

Shaun laughed as I tried to equal his charm.

Again this was a memorable show proving spirit communication live on air. I felt honoured to have been on the same show that James Van Praagh had also frequented. James Van Praagh is a medium I admire very much. It was his voice I recognized giving a message in the show's trailer which advertised the show each week.

It was after that second show that I was asked if I would like a regular two hour guest slot. I just couldn't refuse this offer. After all, my life's purpose is to tell the world about spirit. It seemed the U.S.A was to be included in this equation.

A few weeks later Shaun announced he had a surprise for me. He had remixed the show's trailer and it was now my voice you heard next in line to James van Praagh giving a message. The contrast of my accent to his, made me cringe a little, but I felt very proud to be associated. I was touched by the thought of both James Van Praagh and myself in such close proximity even though it was on tape. This was now the second trailer in which I had starred in the U.S.A, the other trailer being the trailer for the *Psychic Investigator* TV series. At the time I remember being equally excited about this too. I remember receiving an email from the Cineflix film company telling me that my TV episode would be having its debut in New York City and was first being aired to approximately 36 million viewers. I quivered at the thought and began to feel so belittled by the enormity of what was happening. I didn't realize the series was going to be so big. At intimate proud moments like these, what does one do? You call your mother of course! I suppose the response I got from her however, was predictable, having lived with her 'down to earth' humour.

I was all a fluster, as I explained the contents of the email to her. There was very little response as she listened to me as I said nervously,

"Mum, do you realise 36 million people will know my face and know my name?"

But my mother quipped back with her typical Liverpool humour,

"Thank God we've got a different surname."

I could visualize the warmth of her grin down the phone line. I suppose that the child in me, was looking for some sort parental approval or praise, but as usual I left myself open to receive such a 'typical response' from someone with such sharp wit.

It also reminded me that I should keep my feet firmly on the ground. There should be no ego when you work with spirit.

So with my feet firmly 'fixed' and in the months that followed on the Afterlife Show, we had a wonderful array of beautiful moments of spirit communication, all live on air.

Each week there were varying degrees of communication, as sometimes is the case with spirit world. After all, all you had to work with was the voice vibration of the caller, and the 'universal energy' of spirit, of course. There were difficulties for some callers to the show, as they had no previous experience of receiving messages or had little understanding of the process of spirit communication. The difference in culture caused misunderstanding too, on occasion, as some didn't quite understand my accent or the terminologies I used.

But overall, each week was a landmark, and there were some very notable experiences of communication and some exceptionally wonderful shows were produced.

I recall one of my first messages to a young woman.

"You have a sister in the spirit world" I told her.

"Yes ma-am..." she replied.

Then all of a sudden I realized I was visualizing a room on the other side of the world, it was a room in the caller's home.

"I have been taken into a bedroom where there are not one but two children's cots. There are two babies, here in this life that I see. They may be twins (I questioned myself). One child has a good head of hair and the other has none at all." I explained.

"OH MY GAWD! They're my twins!" she screamed. She responded in such a way, which seemed a typical American reply, something which never failed to make me smile as I had very much warmed to the American dialect and idiosyncrasies.

The lady seemed totally shocked by what I had told her. I continued to explain that her sister in spirit was aware of her twins, who had been born after her sister had 'crossed' over and that it was her sister's way of letting her know that she had 'visited' them. It was then when the caller realized that her sister had actually visited her, that she began to cry and thank me repeatedly. She said that she could simply not believe what I had told her.

I discovered that people would call the show with different agendas, not just wanting spirit communication from specific loved ones, but some wanted me to unravel mysteries or circumstances which surrounded the passing of their loved ones too, and all within a six minute radio slot.

One particular lady called the show late. It was 'Mother's Day' in the U.S. I only had time to give her a few sentences, which was a lot less than six minutes, but it was all that she needed. All I said was that she had a son in the spirit world, and I told her I could feel his presence. I could see a clear picture of him in my mind. I told her he was tall and handsome, with dark wavy hair and that he was wearing a flowery shirt and Bermuda shorts.

She gasped.

"He is buried in that flowery shirt and Bermuda shorts," came the reply.

It was one of those show-stopping moments. She said I had given her the best Mother's Day present ever.

Short but sweet, but nevertheless, very 'powerful'. After all, instrumented by the sheer 'power' of his love'.

BEVERLY'S ANGEL

I was particularly moved by an unexpected communication from a young girl's spirit. The caller to the show was named Beverly Schafer-Desmoreau. It unfolded she was the mother of a teenage girl, Leah, who had passed to spirit in tragic circumstances. Her life seemed to have been taken by the hands of others.

I sensed her daughter Leah's spirit instantly, a beautiful soul. I felt a 'power 'of immense presence which equaled the amount of love she wanted to convey, especially to her mother Beverley.

The opening moments of the communication from her daughter just flowed as I sensed her complete being. I could only describe her as a highly evolved soul. Her earthly personality was as Angelic. She in fact was perceived by her mother as an 'Earth Angel'. This was something that Beverly would often call her, she admitted.

Her daughter wanted to tell her something as I heard her shout, "It doesn't matter, it doesn't matter."

She was referring to her last few moments of life, because her mother was unable to be there by her side.

The words were echoing in my mind. Beverly then confirmed that unfortunately that was the case, although her daughter knew and understood very well that it was through no fault of her mother's that she couldn't be there. It was very important for her mother to hear that. I could feel the urgency with her daughter's words in my thoughts. Her daughter didn't want her to dwell on those last moments as her mum had always been there for her during her life, every step of the way.

Once again, this call became one of those most humbling moments. I shed a 'silent' tear as I became aware my cheek was wet. No 'natural' emotion was felt as such, as spirit was, as usual, forever upholding me. I went on to describe a picture of an Angel that Beverley had around her at home. I explained that her daughter's short life here on the earth plane was not just meant to touch Beverley's life as such but to open her mind up to the concept of the Afterlife and the Angels. The purpose of her daughter's life was to touch her 'soul'. Beverley told me her house was full of Angels. I told her that her 'Angelic' daughter was a beautiful old headed child and was 'Beverley's little helper'.

Her daughter had come to say that she had been around her mother more recently, as she knew that the court case surrounding her death was still on-going. And that her mother Beverly had recently moved a photograph of her daughter's to another room and that her daughter's spirit had been 'visiting' her at that time.

Leah's spirit told me that she also knew that her mother had kept a piece of hair, which she often held and stroked.

I told Beverley that her daughter was often stood next to her and in turn her daughter stroked her hair too, and if she hadn't already felt the sensation of her hair being stroked, then she would do so in time.

Leah told me she just wanted to comfort her mum as I could hear her say repeatedly, "Love to you, mum."

At that moment Beverley's Angelic Spirit faded as she returned back to the Spiritual realms.

After the show Beverly contacted me though email to thank me. I felt so humbled to of met her and her Angel daughter, Leah.

I am in no doubt that it was through the influence of Leah's spirit that Beverly would connect with me yet again four years later. In fact, it was when I had just started to pen this book.

Out of the blue and after much searching, Beverly seemed to have tracked me down and sent me a friend request through the social networking website *Facebook*. She reminded me of who she was and of her daughter's communication all those years ago. Beverly's recent connection with me was with perfect timing and purpose. Beverley not only gave me in-depth details of her experience with me, but she had kept the recording of my 'reading' (as she referred to it) and had created a video of photo stills that merged together with my 'voiceover', a recording of my words from the radio show. The photos reflected what was said about her daughter. This was a very beautiful but sad reminder of the works and wonderment of spirit, and of the remarkable 'energy' produced by such a beautiful young soul. There was no doubt that Leah wanted to leave an 'impression' in my book too. Bless her.

LEAH SCHAFER-DESORMEAU

Then there was another enlightened lady caller shortly after, with a particularly unusual request. She said she didn't want any messages from loved ones as such, but said she would like to know who her Spirit guide was. It was a 'first' but never the less a request to spirit all the same.

As I went deep into thought, I visualized a Native American Indian, and yet I had doubts about my 'vision'. It seemed too obvious, when taking into consideration American history but I heard my guides tell me that her guide belonged to the Sioux Indian tribe. This convinced me I wasn't wrong.

"You have a Native American Indian Spirit Guide, but of the Sioux tribe so I believe." I told her.

"Oh, oh! My goodness! I have Native American Indians in my family line." she said. "My ancestors were actually of the Sioux tribe. It is SO good to know that, Angela. My, my... you're such a blessed woman!" she said. I thanked her.

You always have to deliver what you receive no matter how obvious or un-obvious it seems. You have to have trust in yourself, but most of all trust in your 'helpers'.

The vibrations on the airwaves were definitely riding high that night and also in the weeks and months that followed.

The American people were warm and welcoming. I got used to the Americans with their slang phrases, terminology and the slight cultural differences. It was all so different to their English counterparts responding to my findings with a reserved 'yes' or 'no' answer. It was in such contrast that Americans would often choose the more dramatic "OH MY GAWD!" response, as a way of confirming the details I relayed to them.

This particular response made me smile and lightened my heart each time. Bless them.

MURDER ON AIR

It was not unusual to have callers to the show who had loved ones that had passed in tragic or mysterious circumstances. They in turn wanted and hoped for some kind of closure, maybe an answer in unravelling the mysteries surrounding their loved ones' deaths. To no real surprise, they often did receive some of what they were searching for, as it was all a part and parcel of the healing process of the 'Gift' of Mediumship.

One particular evening, I unraveled one of the most tragic cases of all, live on air.

The six minute limitation of the caller was broken by the pure intense spirit intervention, all for the sake of a repenting father in spirit. So it seemed.

I began by welcoming a woman named Glenda. That's

all the information I was given, her name. The relative she wished to receive communication from was not mentioned as sometimes was the case. I instantly told Glenda that her mother and father were in spirit.

"Yes, that's right honey," she said. "I have my mother and father who have crossed over."

I told her it wasn't in recent years that they had passed but it was ten, twenty or thirty years ago now, as I had sensed a distant feeling in the length of time.

"There is something about their passing," I said. "I believe they passed over within half an hour of each other, in very tragic circumstances." There seemed to be a prolonged silence before she explained the reason and told me I was right.

"I must tell you that my father shot my mother, and the cops shot my Dad, hence them dying within half an hour of each other."

I could hear Shaun in my head set take a sharp intake of breath as he too was shocked by her response.

I began to feel her father's presence quite strongly, so I asked Shaun not to call this communication to an end. I 'sensed' by the intensity of its power, it was going to be lengthy communication.

I went on to explain that I felt her father's spirit, who had an overwhelming presence with me.

I continued to say. "I sense your father wants to communicate with you. His energy is powerful and strong."

I could hear her father pleading for forgiveness, and I relayed his plea.

"He is begging for forgiveness, he wants you to understand if you can. And in some way, shape or form, forgive him, if possible."

I began to explain that his soul could not progress and move on until he had at least some understanding of his 'plight' here on the earth and as part of the 'conditions' which now adhere in Spirit.

Having or grasping an understanding is a form of forgiveness and in some way, it will enable to set his soul free from the torment. I sensed he had waited so long for the opportunity to communicate this.

I continued to say. "I sense this is the first time that your father has been able to communicate since that tragic evening. He is begging you for forgiveness."

I repeated this as I could hear him so pensively clear, begging, "Please forgive me." He continued to cry.

I could feel myself having to hold on to my own emotions trying my best to keep them in check.

I began to sense more of her father's emotions, feelings of remorse and anxiety.

"I... I do... I do forgive him... I do forgive... I understand now." she stuttered and cried.

"Although it was a long time ago, I can tell you that your father is aware that you have only just received some sort of counselling over the prolonged emotional pain and turmoil surrounding the event, something which has silently been hidden and eaten away at you all these years."

"Yes... Yes... Oh my God!" came the reply.

I was aware I was being totally instrumented.

Then the tragic event started to unfold in front of my eyes in a 'vision'. I carried on talking.

"I sense that what your father did, was totally out of character." I continued....

"On the evening in question, he was fuelled with alcohol. He just 'flipped' but he was a good man at heart. I 'feel' that he loved his family dearly."

My 'vision' became stronger I started to describe what I could 'see' as I told Glenda that she was in her teens at the time and on that particular evening she was outside of her house in a friend's car, when she heard the first gunshots. And that she began to panic as she realized her sister was inside the house. Glenda had feared for her sister's life and made attempts to go and get to her, but she was held back by her friend. And that she was in an extreme state of panic, helplessness and distress. Those feelings had lingered and haunted her for years.

I could hear Glenda gasp at each statement I made. It took her breath away. Again, there was a long silent pause.

I continued as I 'received' more.

"I get a great sense of remorse from your father. It was a case of him fearing the loss of his marriage. That's what it was all about." I proclaimed.

Glenda began to sob. "You're right, so right, that's what it really was all about."

"I do forgive him," she said "I understand now. Please tell him I forgive him." she begged.

"He knows that now," I told her. "He wants to thank you so much and sends you so much love and healing thoughts."

I reassured her that his communication reflected only pure love for her, but at the same time; it held the deepest remorse and regret. To my surprise her father continued to communicate.

"Your father is talking... of someone called Benny." I added.

"Benny is my brother." she replied.

"Your father is so proud of you all and of what Benny has achieved."

"Benny owns a very successful business." she added.

"Your father has watched over you and the rest of the family, all these years and has followed your footsteps. Your father wants to send love to Benny, and says that he will be drawing close to him as there is something coming up in November. He is letting you know that he will be around at that important time." I said, as the presence lingered.

The reply came back and apparently her Bother Benny was due a heart operation in November.

"Your father will be there watching over him, of that I have no doubt."

Glenda's and her father's time together on air was drawing to a close.

It was then that there had been a great realization for both Glenda and her father's spirit. Not only had they gained reconciliation, but also some consolation and an immense measure of healing, during what seemed an extra-long process in the show. Her forgiveness and understanding had now enabled her father's spirit to transpire to the appropriate realm in peace. Most of all it was bringing that peace of mind' that was paramount to Glenda's healing process too.

As it turned out, that particular scheduled 'six minute slot' dominated the whole hour of the show. DJ Shaun had a duty to spirit to let the powerful link of communication flow right through to the end regardless of a scheduled time.

Shaun ended the show by reassuring and thanking

Glenda for her part in the communication, recognizing the difficulties and the emotional pain it must have caused her but he also recognized the therapeutic spiritual counselling and healing that took place via the spirit realms as the healing power of the communication to both Glenda and her father became apparent.

DJ Shaun wound up the show with a statement, saying that it had been the most riveting show recorded to date. I was left feeling humbled once more and I thanked all those people and souls involved.

My radio work which initially seemed a challenge had become a benchmark in discovering the many aspects of my gift's capabilities. A pure learning curve, educating not only callers and listeners but also myself, a continued learned soul.

I had overwhelming feedback from the American people and the worldwide listening audience. This response reflected in the number of emails and messages I received after each of my shows. The radio show was itself a wealth of transpiring knowledge. The messages were not only of love and hope but also of encouragement, forgiveness, advice and recompense. Each one of the messages accepted and validated to a high degree.

It was a raw, live show. This long distance spirit communication via satellite was founded due to the small rehearsal involving another man from Iran some years before. It is obvious that the power of God's spirit can work within and beyond the power of technology as its infinite power is greater than the universe

TWELVE LITTLE ANGELS

Over the years I have given many messages from war heroes, young men, grandfathers and forefathers who had gallantly served in the Forces. It wouldn't be unusual to 'see' them appear, donned in each of their regimental uniforms knowing that they would have been injured and shot during war time combat.

It has only been in recent years where I have begun to receive communication from spirits of young men, that have been shot and killed. Not in a war zone, but on our streets.

Sadly, this is a reflection of today's violent society in which we live. My first such victim came as a complete shock to me. It was a young man's spirit who induced a new feeling within me. It was a case where I had to take on board the sheer feeling of the sudden blast of a fatal gunshot wound.

I was on a 'house call' several years ago, to a young woman named Amanda who lived in Smith's Wood in Birmingham.

I made myself comfortable sitting alongside her on her couch. I felt drawn to look at the empty armchair beside me. Almost instantly, I had a 'vision' which I began to describe to her and say.

"I can see a young black man sitting in that chair there." I said as I pointed.

Amanda looked at me with a surprised look on her face. "What do you mean?"

I had to explain how I worked and that I would often see 'visions' of people, whether they were living or not as sometimes is the case.

"I can see a young black man sitting on that chair, with his legs out stretched, his arms folded, holding his chin deep into his chest, laughing heartedly and watching TV."

"Yes..." she answered. She'd listened attentively with a blank expression on her face but it was understandably one of shock.

I continued. "He's wearing a pork pie hat and rectangular sunglasses."

She gasped and said, "That's my partner who's dead."

I continued to describe what I could see. "He often sat

71

in that chair out stretched like that. He's laughing heartedly. He seems to be watching the TV. In fact, he's watching *The Simpsons.*" My vision was clear and complete. He had certainly made me aware of his presence.

"I just can't believe how you have described him. I'd heard you were good but this is mind blowing. I've got something to show you." she said.

Amanda left the room and returned with a framed photograph of her partner wearing his pork pie hat.

"That's him," she said as she handed me the photograph "he often wore rectangular sunglasses with that hat."

I held on to the framed photograph and continued to connect with his spirit. I told Amanda that I sensed he was a bit of a character and was known to a lot of people by his nickname. I began to hear a name being called but felt I did not quite grasp it.

"His nickname sounds like Alf, is that correct?" I asked Amanda, as the sound of his voice began to materialize in my thoughts.

"My God, his nickname wasn't Alf, but Alpha in fact… but I would shorten it at times." she replied.

"Alpha has crossed over recently…" I said and she forced a smile and nodded.

She went on to add, "He always sat in that chair, and

The Simpsons was one of his favourite programmes. I never understood what he got from watching it." she said, smiling wryly.

It was just then when I realized how he had passed. It made us both jump, as I got the sensation of a blast in my chest. I demonstrated this with my hand and with a force. "Whatever way he passed, there was a blast in his chest."

She then confirmed my alarmed feelings.

"He was shot..." said Amanda.

I realized then that I had felt a total new sensation which I had never felt before. But I knew the reason for why; it was because his spirit was so close and that I needed to know for a purpose about the conditions in which he had passed.

I found myself repeating the action with my hand as I could hardly believe what I had felt. And wondered why I should feel the action with such intensity. I told her that I could hear him saying something like, "She had a lucky escape."

He was referring to Amanda on that fateful night.

"I did. I was meant to go out with him that evening, but the baby sitter let me down. I would have been in the car with him when they shot him." she cried.

I held her hand and told her that Alpha actually knew who had shot him and that he knew that person was now serving a prison sentence. I could hear Alpha saying he was sorry for causing her so much trouble and heartache, and that he loved her. "He wants to send love to you and his family, but he is talking of his 'little girl' here, who he loves dearly." I explained.

"Yes, it's his little girl, our daughter Milleeka." Amanda replied

"He tells me that he used to sit and read her stories at night, and says something about a star in the sky?" I quizzed.

"He always read her a bed time story."

"And he still does." I said, interrupting her. It was one of those moments when I wondered why I had spoken so spontaneously. Again I'd said something strange, yet made sense to her.

"The strange thing is, since Alpha's passing my little girl wakes up in the morning and often tells me that her daddy has read her a story the night before. I put it down to the fact it was one of the special moments with him, that she really enjoyed and misses so much. But only the other day she said something even stranger to me, again she said that daddy had read her a story and then she asked why daddy had no legs. Why was that?" Amanda asked me.

I explained to Amanda that it wasn't her daughter reflecting on her own memories so much, or a case of wishful thinking. It definitely was her father's spirit reading her a story.

"Alpha's spirit felt the need to manifest partially, purely because he wanted to initiate a chain reaction for your daughter to ask this question and in turn to let you know that he really was visiting her." I said.

This wouldn't be the first time I had heard of such a thing. It was Spirit's way of enlisting a child to relay a message of communication. Children are often very receptive and will give and demonstrate great evidence of the spirit world.

"God, that's amazing." said Amanda. It gave Amanda great comfort knowing that Alpha was still around visiting his little girl. Amanda's realisation seemed to light up her face. She started to explain the reason why Alpha would mention 'the Star in the sky.

"He must know that it was my way of explaining to our little girl, where her daddy has gone. As I had told her, he had gone up to heaven in the sky and that he was now a star watching over her." Amanda then told me her daughter would often look up to the sky at night to see her Daddy.

Just then I had another vision of a tall thin gangly looking man, entering the room through the patio doors and approaching Alpha sitting in his chair. I sensed he was calling Alpha names but in a fun way. I described this to Amanda and she grabbed my arm. "That's my Dad you're describing. He would have had a 'bit of banter' with Alpha. He had a great sense of humour."

I then sensed her father's presence just as strongly too. I sensed he had passed with a condition of the lungs. I also heard him say something about his 'little angels's. I passed on these thoughts to Amanda.

"What is he referring to?" I asked.

By the look on her face I could tell it had a strong, significant meaning.

"Little angels!" she screamed. "Oh my God! My dad always called us kids that...his little angels." she confirmed.

I interrupted and said alarmed, "TWELVE! Twelve of them?"

Amanda laughed through her tears and said, "Yes, twelve. There are twelve of us in the family. That's what he used to call us kids, his twelve little angels."

She also told me that she and her brothers and sisters had placed twelve little ornamental Angels on his grave, representing each of his twelve children.

It was obvious by the warmth of her father's character and by the strength of his presence that he had achieved a poignant message, conveying his love to his family but especially to his twelve children, aware of the gesture they had recently made in his memory. These kinds of gestures do not go unnoticed.

Amanda had not only been blessed once but twice, knowing that she had received a double dose of communication and a double dose of love on that day.

I have never forgotten the intensity of Alpha's visit, his pork pie hat, and the fact it was the first street shooting that was drawn to my attention in a spiritual sense.

It was several years later when I began to gather my memoirs to write this story, I had an unexpected encounter with Amanda's loved ones once again.

As I began to set about writing Alpha's story, I thought it would be nice touch to have a copy of the photograph that I'd been shown during his 'visit' but I hadn't seen Amanda since and I wasn't a hundred per cent sure if I'd remembered her name correctly as years had gone by since I first met her.

However, I strongly felt I needed to obtain a copy and those in spirit understood my need. The first thing I did was to test run the series of events past a number of people as friends and family would often sit and listen to my favourite events. My children more so, they needed very little coaxing, but after all they were used to me. I would rebound my thoughts as they would often jog my memory if I'd forgotten a detail or two.

I was still unsure of the name of Alpha's partner at the time of penning this book, as no one else had remembered either in this case. So I spent some time looking through old diaries in hope I could find an address as I knew which area they lived but found nothing. I could still visualize where they lived, which was in a cul-de-sac off a main road in the

Smith's Wood area of Birmingham. The problem was that it was on an estate ,where all the houses looked very similar. The spirit world knew I longed to get hold of this photograph.

It was the very next day I was woken by a man's voice in my ear, so loud.

"It's Amanda… go now!" the voice commanded. It made me jump.

I knew the man's voice was referring to my recent nagging doubt. It was then I had no doubt at all that her name was definitely Amanda, but I also knew I had to make a visit to the area that day, as the man's voice ordered me to go 'now'.

It was nothing unusual for me to receive communication on waking and then acting upon it, although I didn't get the chance to follow it through until later that day. Still the voice echoed in my head several times, until eventually I had space and time to drive to Smith's Wood in search of Amanda and the much wanted photograph.

I found that the main road that I'd visualized quite easily but was baffled and disheartened by the number of cul-de-sacs leading off it and my added confusion was that the houses looked far too similar. I was almost giving up on the trail when I called in at a local shop to buy a drink. I noticed a gang of youths, a dozen or more of them were hanging around outside. The sight of them was quite intimidating but I thought nothing of approaching them as I felt compelled to.

As I approached them they looked at me in an alarmed manner. Almost surprised that I, a woman on her own, would have dared to step into their space and territory.

"Excuse me, lads." I said politely "Do any of you remember a young man named Alpha who got shot on this estate a few years ago? I'm looking for his family."

They looked at each other for an answer. I was surprised when one young man piped up with a reply.

"It wasn't few years ago, in fact it was about eight years ago." he said.

"That long ago?" I asked him, as it didn't seem that length of time.

"Yes, I'd heard about it, as I knew his brother."

"Did you know his partner, and does she still live round here?" I asked, not giving too much information away.

I knew deep down I hadn't been sent there that day for no purpose. So I kept reassuring myself.

Then came my answer - the young boy spoke up.

"Yeah... Her name's Amanda but she left the estate some time ago." he said.

I paused for a while as my heart sank, thinking the trail had ended. But he continued, saying, "But her sister only lives across the road, there. There, in the corner house." He pointed in the direction of the building.

I regained new hope; my mission was on again and almost over. I couldn't thank him enough.

It came to no surprise really, to find it was Amanda's sister who answered the door. She looked a bit suspicious towards me at first, but when I explained who I was and the connection I'd had with Amanda.

She looked shocked as she turned and shouted, "Amanda, come here quick!"

Amanda appeared from behind the door, as she just so happened to be visiting her sister that day.

She was totally overwhelmed by my unexpected appearance. She approached me with her hands over her mouth; aghast saying repeatedly that she couldn't believe what was happening.

"Today of all days too!" she exclaimed. Amanda told me that that particular day was the anniversary of her father's death. She then confessed she had been listening in to our conversation at the door and had frozen in disbelief, when she had suddenly realized the added significance to the date and my visit.

It made even more sense to me, as it must have been her father's voice I'd heard that morning. I continued to explain what had happened and the purpose of my visit and asked her if she didn't mind giving a copy of the photograph of Alpha with his signature pork pie hat for my book. Amanda said she would be more than pleased to do so in fact, she thought it more fitting to give me copies of both

Alpha Sey

Alpha and her father's photo too. After all she reminded me that he had communicated and made this ending possible. I've learned over the years that loved ones not necessarily mine, certainly do have a repeating habit of revisiting. Particularly at times when you think they are a distant memory.

Alan Heyden

It was in the same week that I 'met' Alpha. I visited a lady in Coventry. When I began her sitting, I could see a young man dressed in a white tracksuit, wearing a baseball cap and a large thick gold chain which hung around his neck. It had happened again. I was given the same sensation, a blast in my chest. He too had been shot.

At first I had to give myself a 'reality', so to speak. But then again, in my life and my reality, it is very questionable, as I am different from other people. All the same it is hard to believe the coincidence of two young men, who had been shot, communicating in the same week of sittings. A rarity, that both of them could deliver a new type of 'feeling'. I knew it wouldn't be the last time. The coincidences and synchronicities in life will no doubt continue, never ceasing to amaze me, throughout all my days.

I had been taken by surprise once again and so was the woman at the sitting but not for that same reason. She recognized the young man I had described in the white tracksuit instantly, as the young boy who had lived next door to her.

"That's the boy next door," she squealed, "he only died a few weeks ago. What on earth has he come to me for? I never really knew him, but I'd heard he was in a lot of trouble. His poor mother did suffer, but why me?" she asked, as she couldn't understand why he would communicate to her.

Understandably she expected a communication not from a neighbour but from a close relative of hers, as most people often do.

I went on to explain that sometimes a spirit close by can take the opportunity to communicate through the nearest channel. It was as if he had been waiting for me to arrive. The young man's spirit was taking this opportunity to get a message through to his mother. I know that children and young people of the spirit world communicate with a vast amount of energy and power. But it soon made clearer sense to me why.

I was told he was gunned down on his doorstep. The power of his communication made even more sense. People that have passed tragically and suddenly, often leave energy behind at the place where they took their last breath, as residual energy is left behind. It is like leaving a stain on the energy field. The remaining residual energy would enhance conditions, enabling a strong connection and communication.

The young man's presence had stayed strong and long enough to say what he needed to say. There was urgency in his voice. There was a sense of desperation, a desire to make peace.

The woman seemed a little agitated, almost threatened by his presence and his wish to communicate.

"I understand this may have unnerved you a little, but all he wants to say is that he's sorry to his mother and his family for all the hurt and trouble he's caused." I explained that she now had to be the 'messenger'.

"But what if his mother doesn't believe in any of this?" she asked me.

"In my lifetime's experience I have never relayed a message that could not be accepted, as those in spirit know those who will embrace what is said." I reassured her.

On this advice, the lady agreed to pass his message on and was rewarded with a wonderful communication from her beloved husband.

It is in more recent years that I have received communication from even more young men, who have been shot on the streets. Another surprising event was during a visit to Dublin, after a show. It had been arranged for me to give private sittings, individually, to a group of women.

Nothing unusual, until I began a sitting with the third woman in the process. So far, each of the women in turn, had a young son in spirit who had been shot. I had to stop and re-examine what I was receiving, it was more than a coincidence. It then became clear that I was giving sittings to a 'Mothers' Support Group' whose sons had been shot on Dublin streets, in a recent spate of gang warfare. One after the other, they came through with such a power, it equaled the immense feeling of love, that each of them wanted to send to their mothers. It was a remarkably moving experience for all of us.

God bless you all.

JOB DESCRIPTION

I never actually decided to become a 'Medium'. It was never a career choice.

It wasn't until my early adulthood that I'd ever even heard of the word, let alone a word with a possible job description attached to it.

The words 'Psychic' and 'Medium' were not around me as a child. It seemed I related my childhood spiritual experiences to my biblical stories that I had heard on a daily basis. I was comfortable knowing that it was a 'Gift' and I was told in my early childhood, from repeated prophetic dreams, that my gift would later be shared on a worldwide scale. I wasn't prepared to 'come out' about my happenings until my adulthood.

Being a social worker for a number of years was an integral part of my personal and spiritual pathway too. The melting pot of people I met and worked with, during that time helped to mould me, and then there were those who, hopefully, I helped to mould.

I have often been asked if the 'Gift' had ever helped me in my line of Social Work

Naturally, having a deeper feeling of empathy combined with a 'knowing', it was those parts of the' Gift' that would often help build a greater rapport with those in need. Although, at times my psyche would sense a lot of truths, which would inevitably unfold, and it was that side of me, I had to restrain and choose to remain silent. After all, what I knew would be different to what had been recorded or known by others. Understandably, what I knew through spirit would not stand as evidence in any court report.

There was one particular time when my gift was called upon in dire straits during work hours. My car had been broken into and my briefcase which was carrying some confidential papers was stolen. I pleaded with my manager to give me some time as there was one place I wanted to check before an official report was made about the lost files. The Truth was I couldn't tell my Manager I'd had a 'vision'.

I had 'seen' the papers scattered amongst trees on a wasteland which was situated close by the Training Centre, close to where my car had been parked. It wasn't until the next morning that I was able to search for them. Sure enough, all the papers but one sheet where found, amongst the trees on the wasteland just as I was 'shown'. My professional 'skin' had been saved.

Making that leap to become a professional Medium was not easy as it stemmed from a result of difficult circumstances and life changing experiences.

Being a Medium was a pathway which was destined and moulded by my life experiences. A destination that was set in stone from the day I was born, if not before.

To have a strong sense of humility coupled with the 'want to serve' has always been a part of who I am. This was instilled and encouraged in me by my Catholic upbringing and its Ethos. These attributes gained, I find are of essential qualities to being a good Medium. So the string of 'caring' jobs I had actually chosen by myself on my career path was actually part of the training ground and foundations laid down by the plans held in the spirit world, which would inevitably help shape my destiny. I never had any intention to use my 'Gift' as a way of life, let alone a career. Something I personally never planned, the decision to become a professional medium was out of my hands entirely. That decision was made for me by the help of my Spirit Guides who had the first and final say about my future destiny.

All this was happening at a time when I struggled with the advice given to me by Doctors. They were advising me to retire from my job as a Social Worker because of stress and the onset of chronic illness, which came about during a very difficult time in my life.

It took many months to realize I had to listen to what my own body was telling me, as well as my Guides. I couldn't cope with the 'load' I was carrying. My ill health was a combination of number of things. Emotionally I was at rock bottom trying to come to terms with my son's recent disability. The fear of being unemployed was soul destroying. Being a single parent was my biggest pressure. Knowing I was the only breadwinner, I needed to support my family. I felt I was letting them down. The struggle within was great.

I initially took six months off and went back to work, but again I struggled with my health complaints combined with the added stress of my son's own relapses, which made me feel worse.

Again after a return to work I surrendered to another six month break which was to be my last, as an employed Social Worker, which had been my field of work for most of my adult life.

It was during the period leading up to Christmas before the millennium year, 2000. The Doctor had visited me for the umpteenth time to administer pain killing injections due to a series of dilapidating migraines. I remember her making a very stern remark about my health, she said that I should really consider retiring this time.

I was told to think it over, during the forthcoming

Christmas period and to make an appointment with her early in the New Year to inform her of my intentions. She was putting a time limit on things as she said that my health would continue to deteriorate. I was feeling beaten and emotionally insecure; I naturally feared my future prospects.

During my time off work, I as a Medium continued to attend and serve my churches when I could. It was the only part of my life I felt good about and gained something very positive from. I sometimes went to visit a church in hope to receive a duplicated message of some sort about my future, although I was capable of receiving my own.

But I had not received any recent messages regarding my health and my work situation for some time. I somehow knew I had to make a decision but was fighting against it all the same but I still wanted some sort of spiritual comfort with guidance and reassurance that I was doing the right thing.

Seeing to people's needs in respect to bringing bereaved people comforting words with my 'Gift' was not only a need for others but also for me. It was emotionally and spiritually uplifting for me.

During that period in particular, I took every opportunity to grab some spiritual healing, whenever I could, as I knew it helped. My spiritual service to people was not a stress, it was a joy. It has always has been a part of my life in some shape or form throughout the roller coaster of the endeavours of my daily troubles.

I felt it was the only thing I had some control of, and it was no threat to me or to my health. and It was the only thing that seemed to be really helping me.

I could adhere to it wherever and whenever I felt the need, so it seemed. It was my 'Faith' in spirit that kept me going once more.

It was New Year's Eve and I was in bed, getting over another bad migraine. I woke up and looked at the time. I switched on the television and began to watch the build up to the New Millennium celebrations.

I was still feeling drowsy, when I heard the New Year bells ring out. I could hear the fireworks in the street outside and I was waiting for the usual amount of phone calls of family well-wishers to begin. It was then I heard a clear voice in my thoughts. It was Spirit Guide Bridget saying, "Come on now, it's over," in a commanding but encouraging way.

I knew she was referring to my troubles and that nagging decision I had to make about my life, the part about my working life, which I was struggling to make a decision about. I knew then I just had to retire from the stress Social Work. The struggle within me had just ended poignantly with the sound of the Millennium bells coupled with Bridget's voice and her encouraging tones. I felt so relieved.

For a moment in time I felt secure again about my future, the struggle that was within me was now over. I reminded myself that my continued Faith would be all that I needed. Bridget's visit was short as usual but never the less an impact.

I then reminded myself of all the similar messages I had received in my life time, as a child, growing up. Messages referring to my future work but I also remembered a more recent message, a couple of years before.

Once I was told by a medium who I'd met on my travels that I would give up my day job and work for Spirit. At the time I politely agreed to differ with her, as I told her I could not see myself giving up a good career, to go self-employed in any shape or form. "Who in the right mind would do that?" I questioned it, as I told her I had a family depending on me. She did tell me though that it would be life's consequences that would lead me to work for spirit on a daily basis.

I know there are some things we need to know and other things are best left to unfold along life's journey. The Medium at the time did not tell me that the change would come about due to the consequences of a long period of ill health, although it was the key to a transition period, a metamorphosis in my life.

Bridget's millennium message was beginning to draw up a greater picture. It was days later I informed the Doctor I was going to take her advice and retire.

I waited for a dramatic change to happen after the Millennium visit but found myself nearly two years down the line, in the same retired predicament. It was a testing time, although during this time my days were less stressful. I was still suffering chronic illness and unemployment. One bonus was my son's health began to improve slightly, so emotionally I was feeling stronger. But there was a void of 'doubt' waiting to be filled.

During this time, I was also struggling financially. I had to borrow money to survive. Money was never my God. I just needed enough to survive my predicaments, it seemed. I knew from the faith I gained early on in my life that something always did 'turn up'.

Knowing that, God's influence and my Guides always turned up at poignant and significant times and that they were my ultimate saviour and would never let me down. After all, I was told at the turn of the millennium I was beginning new work.

"But where was this work?" I frequently asked myself.

Those couple of years turned out to be a real learning curve. I had to learn to be kind to myself and nurture myself, in such a way so that I could embrace the change to enable myself to nurture the others within my family. It was a 'proud pill' I had to swallow, but I continued to have patience.

Deep down I knew the plans that spirit had for me would happen with perfect timing, but I have to admit my patience was wearing thin.

Until one day, and as usual 'out of the blue', I had

phone call from a travelling Psychic company who had heard about my reputation as a Medium and asked if I would be interested doing some part time flexible work giving demonstrations in large hotels around the U.K.

This was something I just had to say "yes" to, as I had no doubt it was a 'God send'. It answered a lot of my prayers at the time. This invitation was the first step in the direction to my work in the Media and a full time job with spirit.

It was the beginning of a career involving my 'Spirituality' as a day job, using my gift to help and counsel others, spiritually. It was not unlike some of aspects of the social work that had gone before me. This time I was seeing to the Spiritual and Emotional well-being of others.

It appears I started to work for a different 'Governing' body of people, those people of the spirit realms, with God at the Helm. Where could I go wrong?

The demands for my 'Gift' of Mediumship continued and took over my life, filling it with opportunities I could not turn down as they no doubt were created for me. My heightened awareness of spirit escalated. As for my ill health, I managed and cared for it much better, after receiving a lot of healing from both 'sides of the veil'. Now I had found, I had more control over my work load and could work at a pace that was more suitable to my conditions, with only God and his workforce to answer to.

I am blessed, for those early messages have unfolded to be true as I succumb once again to the inevitable power of spirit.

DAYS OFF

Like everyone else, I plan holidays and mark days off on my calendar. Often, when I'm making these plans for a well-earned break, it appears that there are other plans being made in the Spiritual Realms that do not seem to take into consideration those days. It is now understandable that wherever I travel, and wherever I connect with new people, the people of the Spirit world will often take an opportunity to connect to those new people too, regardless of my planned 'days off.'

The people of spirit world have always given me an element of surprise and wonder. Still, after many moments of unexpected interruptions in my younger years and now, nearly all my days, there's always an element of 'wonder'.

The whole of my work load involves 'spirit' in some shape or form, 'pardon the pun'.

There is no such thing as a five day week and certainly no holidays are included, as there is never a planned moment that can be totally mine. It seems I always have to leave room to expect the unexpected.

It was a few days before a theatre show. I had booked a

day off, for a bit of pampering and had booked myself into a local Beauty Salon for a number of treatments. This particular salon had been recommended to me by a client of mine. I arrived at the salon to be greeted by an attractive cheerful lady Beautician with a beaming smile. The beautician's name was Greta. It was after the massage she gave me, when I was feeling rather chilled out that Greta began to polish my nails. We sat opposite one another with the small table between us.

We chatted to one another making polite conversation about our recent holidays. I couldn't help but notice when I looked into her eyes that I sensed a deep sadness. It was just as she held my hand in the process of my manicure, when a communication began to unfold.

All of sudden I could see the outline of a young man's spirit standing next to Greta. His energy began to build up in mind, projecting a picture. I didn't hesitate to question as the conditions seemed right and are always set by those in spirit. The young man needed me to tell Greta about his presence. I found myself interrupting our conversation.

"Greta, I need to ask you something," I began. She paused what she was doing and laid down her tools. She seemed to brace herself as if she sensed something of importance was about to be said.

"Yes..." came the reply, she looked puzzled.

"Do you know I'm a medium?" I asked.

"Yes, the girls in the shop did mention something about that before you arrived." she confessed.

I placed my unpainted hand on hers and said instrumentally, "I can see a young man standing beside you. He looks about sixteen years old. He's wearing a black T-shirt, baggy jeans and a woolly hat."

Greta's facial expression changed with each word. Her eyes began to fill with tears.

"That's my son Russell. He was buried in that woolly hat." she said as she gripped my hand and tightly squeezed it, as if to say thank you.

I was conscious that I didn't want the other customers close by to hear our conversation. I also felt that Russell had crossed over very quickly and unexpectedly with a rare health condition. I told her that he often visited her and that he must have been waiting for me to arrive. I then asked her if she had laid down that day on one of the therapy beds holding her stomach, as in my mind I was 'shown' a picture of just that. She said she had, as she had not felt well, as she had a bit of a stomach upset. I told her that Russell was obviously with her then too. Greta was comforted by his communication and she began to confide in me as she explained that she had had some sort of premonition about her son's death a week or so before the event. She described it to me in detail.

I explained that this sort of premonition was God's way of preparing her, to let her know that his journey here was coming to an end. But it certainly wasn't the 'end' of his life. We both knew that. It became apparent that we shared the same belief. We both knew that he would continue to communicate and bring love and comfort. And this would be the case no matter where she was, at home or at work and whether it was my day off or not.

Russell paid me yet another visit knowing I was going back again for another beauty treatment some weeks later. This time he communicated much sooner than my arrival at the salon. It was as I was driving along just before I reached my destination I was happily singing along to the radio. I suddenly felt compelled to switch the radio off; as I did I heard a young man's voice in my mind say, "My mum has found my clothes." I realized it was Russell yet again.

No sooner had I walked through the shop door, I was met by Greta. She smiled at me, before she could get her words out to say hello. I just had to tell her.

"Your Russell has asked whether you have found some of his clothes. I've just heard him, as I was driving along" I explained.

With a sharp intake of breath Greta replied, "Oh, isn't that strange. I thought I'd given all his clothes away but it is only this morning I've discovered a pair of his jeans hanging alongside mine in my wardrobe. And I have just been to visit his grave this morning before I came into work and sat talking to him as usual. That's uncanny."

"Well think about it this way Greta. Today I'm his voice.

This is his way of answering you back with an instant reply."

Russell visited me again some months later, this time whilst I was at my 'work.' I had been called out to a group of people. My visit had been organized by a woman, who took the first sitting but as I sat down to begin a second sitting with a middle aged man. I saw Russell in my mind's eye, unmistakably. I was taken by surprise by his unexpected visit.

I looked at the man and said quite confidently. "Your Russell's father, aren't you?" I asked.

It was as if I had given the man an electric shock. He literally jumped. He looked startled. "How the heck do you know that? You don't know me from Adam... who told you?" he blurted out looking confused.

My question was a blow to his logical thoughts. He blew out his breath as the shock of what I'd said had clearly taken it away, for a few seconds.

"Russell communicated to his mother a few months ago. I recognized him as he's shown himself to me, and told me that you're his Dad." I said.

The man looked aghast. He sat mostly in silence as his sitting continued with Russell talking about his childhood memories. Russell's father said the occasional 'yes' and nodded. I told him that Russell was often visiting with him too, as he often sat beside him at work, in the cab of the lorry, which he drove long distances.

Russell's dad seemed to sit there swallowing a lump in his throat repeatedly, as he listened motionless. It came to the end of the communication when he told me he used to be a 'non-believer'. I thought he was going to tell me of a spiritual experience that he once had, as people often do like to share their spiritual experiences with me, knowing that I would understand and never ridicule them.

"Oh yes? When did you start to believe then?" I asked him.

"Only since... Errrm... NOW. Since I met you, that is." he said. He stood up and shook my hand saying "I can't believe what I've just heard and I can't begin to tell or describe how I feel." He added.

No description was necessary; the tears in his eyes said it all. Thanks to Russell.

My first meeting Russell may have happened on one of my days off but I'm not complaining. And I never would complain, for I really do feel humbled at the thought that those people in the spirit world choose me to be their channel. I'm their channel, their voice, no matter where I am.

Even when I've booked a holiday , it doesn't mean to say that I'm having a complete or long break from my spiritual connection either, as my spiritual sensitivity is a part of me, an element that has been there since birth and will be 'used' accordingly.

There was one such holiday were I was reminded of this. It was when I was travelling to Barcelona on a coach with my daughter with her team-mates and other parents as part of a football tournament. The idea of sitting upright on a coach for several days and nights was not appealing to me or my ailments. It was a holiday that I would not have chosen for myself but it was only for the purpose of my daughter's talent. It was an opportunity I wouldn't have wanted her to miss. The trip was actually an end of season tournament organized by Aston Villa Girls Football Club, whom my daughter played for. Her interest in football and her talent came as a surprise to me. She was so unlike her sister who was a Champion dancer. It was just something she'd always loved doing, playing with a ball.

Her talents were discovered in the process and she had been scouted a couple of seasons before. I have no doubt my children's talent with football had been influenced by my grandfather Jack's spirit. Jack was a professional footballer in the 1940s and it seemed he had already influenced my son's career, who later became a professional footballer like him. Now Jack was influencing my daughter, so it seemed. My children were not fortunate enough to have met Jack, as he had crossed over many years before they were born but they had heard all about all his glorious football moments and eventful life.

Over the years, Jack had visited me on a number of occasions; his presence had been witnessed and felt many times, particularly at football events. I can't say on this tournament holiday I had any profound visit from jack, although I was half expecting it, but I didn't. Although I knew he'd be watching anyway.

This holiday was eventful to say the least, my daughter broke her toe before the first match and was unable to play, which was great disappointment to her but she enjoyed the holiday nevertheless. She had fun with team mates who rallied round her, taking it turns to literally carry her about from time to time. It was certainly a 'team building' holiday and a chance for the players to really get to know each other.

It was when the tournament was over, which was very much a success as the girls had won the majority of the games, but was beaten on points. They were all on a 'high' all the same and were looking forward to a planned visit to Disneyland Paris on our return journey. At this point, I was feeling physically drained, as the week had taken its toll on me, but I enjoyed the company nevertheless. The thought of the long return journey ahead was daunting.

It was the evening before we reached Paris. I was asleep sitting upright on the back seat of the coach. Suddenly I was woken by a voice of a young teenage boy, whose spirit had appeared in front of me for a few seconds. His presence stayed long enough for me to hear him say, "I couldn't take it anymore."

He disappeared as quickly as he had arrived. I understood him completely, although I was fighting with my tiredness. Still it absorbed me, all the same. By what the boy had said, I was saddened to think that this young boy had taken his own life. He barely looked fourteen years old. Although his visit was short, I had heard what he had said quite clearly.

But why had he'd come to visit me in such an unusual place? I asked myself. It wasn't clear. I settled for the understanding, that maybe some of his living relatives were about to book in for a sitting, once I returned home in a couple of days' time. It wasn't unusual for spirit to make an initial visit before a planned sitting or event, as this had happened many times before.

The actual reason for his visit became more apparent the next day when I was having conversation with one of the team mates' mothers. Her name was Julie; she knew I was a Medium as it was common knowledge to the team and parents. During the week there had been the odd jibe or two directed at me, but all in good humour.

Julie began with a leading question. "You know what you do… how does it happen, and when do you receive messages? Does it happen all the time? Or do you switch it on and off?" she asked me.

Our conversation was leading to a much deeper level as the questions she began to ask about the Afterlife were of a serious nature. She was obviously very open minded and wanted to know more.

"No, I can't switch if off entirely as it is part of me. It is my sensitivity which is the 'receiver', as such. This is a natural 'Gift'... I was born a 'channel' but the connection always happens when I choose to, or when I am asked. But it is all instrumented by 'Spirit'. Although, at times I do receive unexpected communication." I explained.

Then I found myself telling her about my recent visit from the young boy on the coach the night before.

She looked at me and said, "Oh stop! Just stop there! You've made me go all cold. Didn't you know?" she said.

"Know what?" I asked

She explained that a father of one of the Team, who had sat at the front of the coach during the journey, had received a phone call that same night, telling him that his best friend's son who was 14 years old had died, and that he had committed suicide.

I advised her not to mention anything to anyone, as it was all too soon, as emotions were far too raw to pass on any message. I began to understand more of the purpose to his visit, as it instigated the need for the purpose of the conversation we were lead into.

Then Julie the young mother asked me my views about suicide.

"Some people say that if somebody commits suicide they don't go Heaven and as a result they are stuck somewhere in a place they don't want to be, as a punishment. For they have committed the ultimate sin against God by taking their own life. Is that true or is that not the case?" she questioned.

"No certainly not."

"What really does happen, then?" she asked.

I told her that from the knowledge given to me from the Spiritual Realms and from what I have learned through my own experiences of spirit, such people who do such a thing aren't punished at all. In fact they and their emotions are healed in the process, once they cross over to the other side. They, like everyone else with illnesses and ailments, become healed and become whole again. They are the same as everyone else, nurtured by God and their loved ones in spirit.

I continued to tell her that scientific studies have now shown that suicidal thoughts are actually a symptom of depression, and depression is like any other illness that leads us to cross over to the other side.

Suicide is an act we didn't understand some years ago. And those people who did such a thing were often frowned upon and supposedly dammed, and so was their family remaining. According to their faith, it often carried a great stigma.

Sadly, such attitudes, through lack of knowledge and ignorance, still exist today. We still do need to educate people about suicide and the reasons behind it. This young boy's act was no sin. He would be given God's loving care like everyone else. Such people are handled with God's greatest of care. They are granted the understanding as part of their healing process, when they reach the other side. They may be taken to what I call and know of the 'healing rooms' which is something like the equivalent of our hospitals here. Where they may stay for a period of time to heal and then follow into the spiritual realms or even be sent back down to earth accordingly like some other souls. I am a great believer in reincarnation too, I told her. We should help to heal his spirit too with prayers and loving thoughts.

"What are the healing rooms, and how do you know there are such things?" Julie asked.

I began to explain by telling her about an experience I once had, that convinced me of the healing rooms' existence.

I told her this is something I had learned about first hand. The phrase 'the healing rooms' was first given to me at the beginning of a young man's sitting when out of the blue I said to him, "You've been to the healing rooms, so I believe."

He looked as much surprised as I did. I knew my instant words and thoughts were being totally instrumented. To accompany the phrase I just happened to mention, that I could see a 'vision' of the young man walking along corridor with several doors leading off, it was if he was being led into a particular room. The room was full of piercing light, and as he lay down on a bed, I could see and sense that he was being surrounded by a group of people who I 'knew' were familiar to him in some way. I described what I 'saw' to him, and his jaw dropped.

"That's it, that's exactly it... exactly what I saw." he said, almost screaming.

"It's all connected with a motor bike accident." I said

He went on to explain that he had had a motorbike accident eighteen months before and he had lain in a coma for weeks. He told me that what I was describing to him was exactly what he 'saw' and had experienced so vividly in a so called 'dream' during the time he was comatose. The purpose of his visit to me, was to find some answers as to 'why' he had survived, when all the odds were stacked against him and to find an explanation to his strange 'dream'.

Little did he know he had actually received 'healing from the other side', a haunting phrase that sounded all so familiar to me.

The reason why he had been sent back to the earth plane, was to let people know about the existence of the higher realms of spirit. I told him that within the process of time he too would do some spiritual work; his life had been saved for that purpose too.

I had hoped this had answered Julie's questions about suicide and the healing rooms.

"That sounds amazing… but it does not make sense to me. Although I do find some things hard to believe, I suppose a lot us want our very own little piece of evidence."

It wasn't long before Julie had her 'own little piece of evidence' some weeks later, in her very own sitting with me. She received a personal message from her father in spirit. Julie had now had also become another messenger of her new found knowledge of Spirit and gained a crucial understanding of suicide. She now would be able to relay the true understanding of the young boy's passing to whoever she felt comfortable with, and spread the 'word'.

JOSH

A young lady named Marion, who happened to see an article of mine in a newspaper, phoned me and booked a sitting. Apparently she said she felt drawn to the newspaper, and my name seemed to leap out at her. I'm more inclined to say she was 'led' to me, in reflection that would be most true to my understanding of the 'fated' circumstances.

Marion explained that she would be travelling some distance, to visit her sister who happened to live in my local area and asked whether her 'reading' as she called it, could take place at her sister's home. She said she was fairly new to 'this kind of thing' and that in fact, I would be 'a first' for her. Even though she said that she had gathered some understanding of the process, it became apparent that she didn't know as much as I initially thought.

I picked up on Marion's psyche instantly as I sat down with her and her sister.

Marion came across as a thoughtful, sensitive, bright and breezy kind of a girl. She seemed little bit confused about what to expect, as she seemed surprised that I didn't have any cards with me, as she asked me where they were.

I explained about my 'gift' being natural, and that I didn't need any cards as such and that I was not only psychic, rather a medium and a visionary. I tried to explain in simple terms what I do.

I asked her just to sit and relax and to send up loving thoughts to all her loved ones in spirit and let the process of communication begin, as I had already prepared myself for 'work' as usual beforehand.

I began to tell her that I could sense a Grandmother in spirit, on her mother's side of her family, who was now drawing very close to her. A 'vision' of her grandmother appeared in my mind. Her Grandmother was holding a little baby boy.

"There's a little baby boy in spirit," I said, "Who your grandmother seems to be looking after. I believe it's your little boy."

Marion screamed "Oh my God!" she couldn't hold back her tears and began to cry. At the same time she seemed lifted, as she nodded in agreement and told me that she simply couldn't believe what I had told her.

The confirmed truth of the words, as I continued to tell her that her little boy was eight months old when he had crossed over, and that he looked perfect in every way. I told Marion that her Grandmother had come to collect him and she was now looking after him. I heard her grandmother call the name Josh.

"Who is Josh?" I asked Marion.

Marion gasped and said, "That's his name... that's my baby."She cried.

Marion grabbed her sister's hand who had sat silently crying with her. She had difficulty speaking through her sobs, muttering, and thanking me, as if that was all she was expecting me to tell her.

" All I needed to know is, that someone was looking after him," she said. "I'm so glad to hear that. And to know that it is my Grandmother that has him now, who I love so much too. Thank you so much, you're amazing."

In my vision, Josh appeared to be wearing a white baby grow with an emblem of a teddy bear on his chest. Her little boy looked beautiful and perfect in every way, but I sensed that there had been something wrong with his head. This was the condition that caused him to cross over, I was convinced of this. I also sensed that he had passed in a hospice and had received months of treatment beforehand.

I relayed all of this to Marion. She was clearing suffering from very raw emotions as Josh had not long passed. She confirmed all of what I had said was true, but admitted she was still finding it very hard to absorb the communication, as she had been expecting some kind of card reading.

Marion repeatedly thanked me but amidst her grief she seemed elated knowing that her baby Josh was being looked after by members of her family.

I'd never witnessed so much elation and gratitude expressed during someone's heartache. She had obviously gained great comfort. It was as if she wanted the world to share it with her but most of all she wanted her husband to share this comfort.

"I wish my husband Neil could be here and witness all this. I know that learning that Josh was okay and being looked after would help with his grief, but I'm afraid he doesn't believe in any of this at all," she explained. "He doesn't talk about Josh as much as I do. Maybe he'd feel better if he knew about this; it may help him to talk more. I suppose that's his way of handling things." she said, examining his reasons and actions.

I then felt I should share something with Marion about grief. "Two such people as yourselves who have lost a child often grieve in different ways and at different stages, and are often not 'on the same page' with their grief. Each one of you can feel isolated although you have each other but sometimes a belief system often helps. Maybe one day Neil will start to believe in time, let's hope so."

I just felt those words were being instrumented, as if I knew one day he would believe.

No sooner was the sitting coming to an end and Marion had already asked what length of time I would recommend before the next sitting. It was obvious that she couldn't get enough of her experience.

I explained that people come to me on a regular basis but at various times and for various reasons. Often they visit me when things are happening in the lives and they need the comfort to know, that their loved ones are aware of their situation too. In other cases, they may require help and advice, a 'real' answer to the troubles that they may be experiencing. Sometimes, they just need the comfort and peace of knowing that their loved ones are still watching over them and are still with them in some way, or they want to ask their loved ones to bring them the help they need. I know that spirit will always give us an answer and will certainly send us what 'we need' even if it's not necessary what 'we want' at times.

It was about a year or so later near Christmas time when Marion came to visit me at my home. She seemed to float in, in her normal breezy manner. She sat down rubbing her hands together almost in excitement, bracing herself for what was in store. It appeared that she seemed to be expecting the same amount of comfort, as she had gained at her first sitting.

Each sitting is unique as you never know what level of communication you will receive. A good communication involves all of the elements playing an equal part in receiving the vibration, which is set within certain conditions and will flow accordingly.

Within minutes of a polite conversation, I had my first 'vision'.

This time I saw Josh as the little toddler he had grown into now, as they continue to grow in the Spirit world. He was now able and old enough to walk. I became in awe of him as in the 'vision' he'd walked across my living room, toddled up to Marion and placed a small toy motorbike on Marion's lap.

Marion watched the sudden expressions on my face and sat bemused, watching for a while.

"Marion, your Josh is here," I explained, "and is tottering around now."

Marion reminded me that he would have been 18 months old at the time, so it made sense that she should be walking. Her eyes were fixated on my every movement as she could see I was looking at something and she realized it was Josh.

I continued to tell her about my vision. "He's got a lovely head of hair now too. And I don't know why but he has just placed a little toy motorbike on your lap."

Marion glanced down at her empty lap and burst into tears instantly. She was eager to see what I could see, I could tell that.

"I can't believe this," said Marion looking at her empty

lap "I have placed a little toy motorbike on Josh's grave, just this week."

I explained any gesture or gifts we present to our loved ones in spirit, they are aware of and will precipitate that gesture. They do receive them and are often 'mentioned' or 'presented' during a future communication.

For those children who can't communicate verbally as they are too young or incapable, their words in thoughts come through with the help of their own guides and helpers or loved ones.

Josh seemed so excited as through his eyes I could see what he wanted to convey. He was showing me a 'vision' of what I sensed was his Daddy, who seemed to be busy changing a wheel on a motorbike.

"Does Josh's daddy have a motorbike and has he been changing a wheel lately?" I asked.

Marion had grasped and confirmed that he had changed a wheel in the last few days.

"This is Josh's way of letting you know he was standing there watching his daddy that day." I said.

By this time Marion was in floods of tears.

"I can't wait to tell him. I just wish he would believe. I will certainly tell him all this. I know it would help him," she said referring to Josh's father, Neil. "But as much as he wants to believe, he needs his own proof. He needs to hear it from you. He needs to be here." she said in a disheartened tone.

At this moment, I was compelled and instrumented to tell Marion to ask Neil to look under the left sleeve of his motorbike jacket, as there was a hole there. That would be all the proof he would need to believe.

Why did I say that? I questioned myself but I just knew why, somehow. It was just one of those moments. Such moments as those that have been part of my persona all my life but still have the ability to shock me, even now.

"Oh I don't know about that..." Marion said, questioning and dissecting the strange remark I'd just made, "His motorbike jacket is fairly new."

"Sometimes Marion," came my reply "I just have to say things, I don't know why but I do. I have said strange things since I was a child, things that end up meaning a lot more."

Just then I felt compelled to make another 'strange' comment.

I grabbed Marion's arm. I did it as if I needed her full attention to what I was about to say which I felt was of great importance.

"You will be rejoicing on June 2nd."

Marion's facial expression changed for the worse.

"No! I think you may have that wrong. I don't think I'll ever be rejoicing on that day, as that was the day that Josh died."

I apologized to Marion. But as soon as I did so, the voice in thought from my Guide was profoundly louder repeating the same words even clearer. There was no mistake. I knew this date was of importance. I too was thrown a little, if only for a few seconds.

"No, Marion. I've heard the words so clearly again. You will be rejoicing on June 2nd. Please take this with you, as I know it may mean something later. I know what I am about to tell you, does not compensate for the loss of Josh, but there will be another child for you, a beautiful little girl."

I could see that Marion was totally overwhelmed as her sitting came to an end. It all seemed too much for her to

dDigest but nevertheless; she was a joy to watch as she left me. She seemed to be bursting with an emotional uplift, as she said goodbye.

It was just hours later when I received a call from her. She told me about the response from her partner after she had relayed the message about the motorbike jacket. She was almost breathless as she explained.

"I returned home bursting with joy. I couldn't wait to tell him all about Josh, so I then began to tell him about his part of the message. This seemed to stop him in his tracks when I said that Angela told me to tell you about your new motorbike jacket. At first he looked at me as if I'd lost my mind, but I insisted he should go and fetch it.

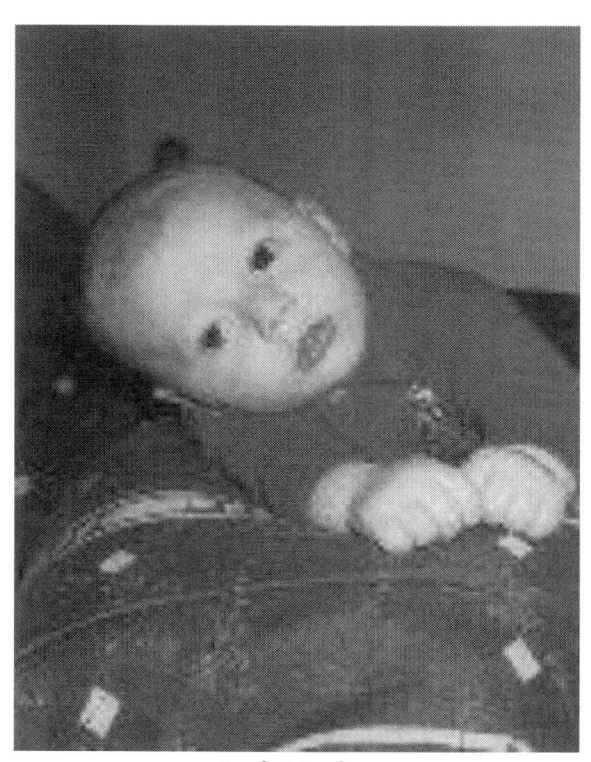

Josh Heelas

He went off into another room but he didn't return. I called to him. But then I found him, sitting crumpled up, in the chair. Cradled up in his arms was his motorbike jacket. At first he didn't say a word; he just stared at me blank. He didn't have to say anything, by the look on his face and the tears in his eyes, I knew what he'd found. He found exactly what you said, a hole under the left sleeve. It took him some time for the words to sink in; he just kept asking me how on earth you knew these things. I told him you were for real and that our Josh was okay and being looked after. I cannot thank you enough Angela, you gave Neil just exactly what he needed, his own proof. He now knows his little Josh is okay. The beautiful part is that he comes to visit his daddy, and watches over him or should I say spends hours standing alongside him, while he mends his motorbike by the sounds of it."

It wasn't Marion's praise that overwhelmed me as much but the sheer beauty of it all: Marion's comfort, Josh's communication and Neil's new-found belief. Who says miracles don't exist? They do and they continued to do so in this case.

It was a year or so later when I received an unexpected call from Marion who seemed so upbeat, as she told me that she had recently given birth to a little girl and the date I had given her in her sitting was very poignant.

She went on to explain, her little girl had to have medical tests to see if she had the same condition that Josh had. It was a worrying time for her. She had to wait for results. The results came in a letter which told her that her little girl was clear from the condition and the letter had miraculously arrived on June 2nd.

Marion told me the word 'rejoicing' was an underestimation. She could not describe how she felt on that day, as her little girl had been given the 'all clear' by the doctors. She was perfectly healthy and heaven sent, just like Josh.

Marion was so comforted and elated she wanted to tell the world about the 'miracles' in her life.

A HARD DAY'S NIGHT

When you think you've done a hard day's work and you've just started to relax and unwind, spirit can choose moments too.

I remember after one afternoon's church service and an evening Show in Liverpool, I had planned to go to dinner with a friend, to a nice City restaurant for an evening meal straight after the show. Quite often you need the allocated time to do the mundane things to get you off the high vibration, spirit takes you on during your work. It can take hours to come down to feeling 'earthly' again. A bit of relaxation is needed, so good food and good conversation is a great way to end such a day.

My friend Marilyn and I arrived at the restaurant late that Saturday evening. To my surprise there were very few people there but the waiter still escorted us to a table. We had just ordered our food, when I couldn't help but notice three men arrive at the restaurant. A small man accompanied by two large burly men either side of him.

The small man was very smartly-dressed and had an air of importance about him. I sensed the two men were his bodyguards or minders. One couldn't help but notice a large gold watch surrounded by diamonds on his wrist, an obvious status symbol.

I couldn't understand why the waiter escorted them to the table adjacent to ours, only a few feet away, when there were so many other tables free. In hindsight, there was an obvious influence going on there.

"Hiya!" said the small man in a Liverpool accent. The other two men just nodded and smiled.

We smiled back. The men were placed so close to our table that they could not help but hear every word we spoke. It wasn't long before they joined in our conversation.

"Where are you from girls, Dudley?" the small man interrupted, trying to pinpoint my friends' Midland accent by mimicking the word 'Dudley' in what he thought was an appropriate dialect.

In an undermining way, Marilyn replied, "No, I'm certainly not from Dudley. I'm from Birmingham to be precise." she said as she beamed with self-pride as she corrected him.

"Oh right. What brings you to Liverpool, then?" he asked.

Before I could give Marilyn any indication to be discreet, it was too late, as in my 'time off,' I like to express the 'other side of me', the side of me that's in tune with the living.

I didn't even get chance to politely kick her under the table before Marilyn piped up and said, "My friend has just finished a Show actually."

"Oh yeah? What kind of show's that?" he asked, looking puzzled. Before I could answer, Marilyn quipped.

"She's a Medium."

I was so was tempted to beat her to the quip with something funny or naughty to say, but she was too 'quick on the draw'.

His response was a typical one.

"Wow that's amazing," then he surprised us by his confession. 'I believe in all that. What can you tell me about me? By the way my name is Harry." he said, as he reached out his hand and shook both ours in turn. The two men beside him again, just nodded.

"I could tell you some things, but please, not now." I said politely, as I looked down at my plate which had just arrived on cue. He understood what I meant and apologized for asking, yet minutes later he asked the same question again. I think the wine he was drinking made him forget.

"Can you tell me anything about me, oh go on!" he pleaded.

He said he'd never had 'a reading' before but was fascinated by the subject. He said that he'd always wanted one, but his busy work load and life denied him the time. Then he asked if many men were interested in the subject as he thought it wasn't a 'macho thing' to do.

Marilyn seemed to urge me with an encouraging look. I then gave in to his needs.

"Something about Alicante?" I said as I asked him with the remaining energy I thought I'd got left.

"My God, I'm going there next week. Of all the places to mention why did you say that to me?"

"And there's something about Hong Kong."

"Jeez, I'm going to Hong Kong in a fortnight's time. You're amazing." he said wide eyed.

I began to 'tune in' as I told him he was a very successful businessman, who had not only one but four businesses. The two men that were sat either side of Harry added very little to the conversation but looked interested in what was being said. They just sat observing and absorbing every word, giving an occasional nod and surprised look from behind the large glasses of wine they sipped. I sensed they were not the most pleasant of characters either, as they were in fact hardened men who were doing a job of minding Harry. He certainly did have an element of charm about him though. A key ingredient to his success, I sensed.

Then my thoughts started to reel. I sensed underneath his small authoritarian stature was a very, needy man. I realized I hadn't come down off the vibration altogether as there was a rise in my senses. Spirit was asking me to work yet again, as I felt his underlying needs which he hid behind his wit and humour, were just too great to ignore.

Harry's cheerful expression changed after the words had struck chords, and then he realized what I was really all about. I got a glimpse of a hurtful look, as he asked me about his sister.

"Look, she's obviously…' crossed over' hasn't she?" I asked. This was confirmed by expression on his face.

"If she chooses to communicate, she will, and if she doesn't, she doesn't. Maybe she will come some other time." I said, almost apologetically, hoping that what I said would dismiss his gentle demands and my feelings that had risen, would diminish.

He was obviously asking and hoping for a sitting there and then, but to be honest I just wanted to eat my meal as I had been looking forward to sitting in this particular plush restaurant all day. It was my reward for a 'hard day's work. So I thought, but maybe there was an 'unexpected reward' to come.

I had only tasted the first few mouthfuls of my food, when I had to surrender to a voice from spirit. I placed my knife and fork down and interrupted the pleasant conversation and laughter, that was being bantered about.

"Who's Jeannie?" I asked Harry.

"My God, that's my sister's name…" he immediately replied.

I smiled at him as if to let him know she was 'here with us'.

He signaled to the two men by waving his hand, indicating to them to be quiet. There was silence, as his late night sitting began. The trail of broken statements from spirit commenced. Harry pieced together all of what I said was a fact about Harry's life and love for his favourite sister.

His sister conveyed to me that she had passed with a cancer condition and that she was emotionally and spiritually very close to him, as they were very close growing up in this life too. She spoke of coming from a family of six children, and Harry being the one she adored.

I told him that he wasn't with her in her final moments, as she was surrounded by the love of her immediate family, her husband and children. Each statement I made was followed by a welcoming 'Yes' as he gasped and swore under his breath.

Jeannie ended her communication by saying that she

was so proud of him and his success but most all the fact he had done lot for children's charities here in the City. He modestly admitted that this was the case. He was obviously a businessman with a big heart.

Harry fighting back the tears took a large intake of breath and then swore out loud repeatedly. It was the only words he knew to express the impact of what he had received and felt. His bad language was forgivable. It was like listening to an outburst by Ozzy Osbourne on a bad day!

"You are so BLEEPING amazing!" he repeated, over and over again. Until finally he was interrupted by spotting three other burly characters he knew, arriving at the entrance of the restaurant. I smiled with relief too, thinking I had given all of what was expected of me and I could continue with my meal.

Although it was Harry's first encounter of such an experience, he obviously didn't want to dwell on his grief, as he chirped up.

"Ah I bet you can't tell me when my birthday is then?" he said as if to try and lighten the mood and test my 'psychic' abilities.

What topped off the evening was my 'reply', which came to me, even louder.

"The day John Lennon died." just seemed to trickle out of my mouth. It was like shooting a bullet out of a gun to watch his reaction.

"My God! Of all the things to say to me! John Lennon is my hero. You are looking at the biggest John Lennon fan here. I was totally gutted when he died, he actually died on my birthday!" he seemed obviously elated by the 'entertainment' I had given him.

Then three men arrived and approached Harry and his minders, as they joined them at their table. I sensed their 'energy.' and I began to feel a little uneasy with their presence. I indicated to Marilyn it was time to leave. I stood up with my Bill in hand and said our goodbyes. Harry insisted in swapping each of our business cards. As we did, he snatched my Bill out of my hands and insisted on paying. It was a nice gesture from him and it was my little reward from spirit, I thought.

Harry's desire for a message was very much needed, as he had not 'received' anything from his sister before, let alone spirit. Spirit always knows best, for they had found a perfect space and time in Harry's busy Business schedule although a slight interruption to mine, as usual, but not without a complimentary meal or two.

INTERNATIONALE

Space and time is 'set' for us all, along a journey of self-discovery. It seems that no matter how much we plan, there are always heavenly 'interruptions', which some people recognise and others clearly do not. But for those who believe, their confirmation will come from the coincidences, synchronicities, the signs and symbols reminding us of God's force that is present in all creation.

I always say people are 'sent' to me, for they are sent by spirit with perfect timing and space, no matter how near or far.

Over the years I have been blessed to 'receive' a melting pot of people, some that have travelled many miles to meet me. I feel honoured and warmed by the fact that there seems to be little 'pockets of me' all over the world now, or shall I say 'pockets' of my 'communication'.

Those international calls and sittings reflect a true representation of all our loved ones in the spirit world; no matter what religion, creed or colour.

They are all there, united in the spirit world. If only more of that 'union' could be reflected here on the earth.

I was a little surprised at a telephone call as, the voice on the other end said;

" Hello my name is Oyin, but people call me Honey." said a young sounding woman with a French accent. I smiled, at the beautiful French tones in her voice. She reminded me of my spirit guide Therese.

Honey explained she had seen me on TV on the *Discovery Channel*, at her home in Paris and would like to arrange a sitting in person.

She said she had visited London often, and to travel the Midlands would make little difference. So we made arrangements to meet.

To make the final part of her journey less complicated , we arranged to meet in a Hotel in Birmingham's City centre.

It was on that bright summer's day whilst driving into the city, a 'surprise' picture kept flashing up in my mind. The picture was of an African woman in some kind of traditional dress it seemed. She was wearing a bright yellow patterned garment and matching headdress. When I 'saw' it for the first time I thought it odd, as I had no clues to who she was and as to why she had shown herself to me.

Then, it dawned on me that this lady had a connection with Honey. I sensed that this lady was Honey's mother, who was in spirit.

It became clear that Honey was French, but of African descent. The repeated flashing of the 'picture' gave me confidence to think that.

As I approached the ring road to the city centre, I became alarmed. There was extraordinary numbers of police cars and fire engines whizzing past with sirens blasting. I felt an extreme atmosphere of intensity. Something was happening in the city centre that day. I saw a number of roads, cautioned off with tape. Shops were being emptied. People were spilling out onto the pavements. Someone told me that apparently there had been some kind of chemical spill, but there was confusion too, as others thought it could be a bomb scare.

Honey phoned me saying she was still at New Street Railway Station. I told her to wait there and not to worry as the city was more of a maze with what was going on. Then my phone went dead before I could say anything else.

When I arrived at New Street Station, I found myself being completely 'guided' amongst the many hundreds of people. I saw two women and made a beeline to them, as I walked up behind them I called out Honey's name.

It made her jump a little "Oh my goodness, how did you know it was me?" she asked. She explained she had brought a friend with her.

I smirked and shrugged my shoulders with open arms and glanced up above. She understood my non-verbal gesture. She beamed with a warm smile.

I couldn't wait to tell her what I'd already received.

"You have a mother in spirit" I said.

"Yes! Yes!" she said with delight.

She reached into her handbag and pulled out a photograph to show me. It was of two women African in traditional dress.

"You saw my mother? So which one is she?" Honey asked, in a testing but understandable way.

I pointed to the lady in the yellow patterned dress, she squealed again but this time she started to cry.

"Come on, let's go and find that quiet place to see what she has to say." I told Honey.

We couldn't get to the hotel because of the chaos on the streets. It seemed they were trying to shut down the whole of the city centre and evacuate people throughout, well at least the roads which we could see.

Time was of the essence, so we scurried in to a small café and settled in a corner with a photograph in hand, and her mother's spirit in tow.

Honey came across as a very warm and sensitive young lady. She sat attentively listening to her mother's every word. She examined each remark I made and asked me to repeat myself, not for any lack of understanding, just to feel the closeness of her mother once again.

Her mother spoke of Sierra Leone as that is where she had lived, and died. She was very proud of her daughter Honey, as she had escaped the troubles of her war-torn township and knew that she had made a new life in France. She spoke of Honey's recent promotion regarding her teaching post too. She also mentioned her beautiful granddaughter, Honey's child and said that she knew Honey had married a wonderful French man. Honey's mother seemed overwhelmed with pride; this was reflected by the strength and determination of her communication. Honey was just enthralled with it all.

Honey returned the compliment by inviting me to France. She said she was simply moved and so touched by the whole process. It seemed most important for Honey to know that her mother's spirit knew of the struggle she had once had and what she had achieved since.

For me it was the timing and space most of all. No chemical spill or bomb threat was going to deter her mother's spirit or any of us that day.

I remember going home and sharing some of the 'startling' events of the day with my son, who often listens to my 'adventures'. He listens intently and does show serious interest in all I do, although he would always follow up whatever I say, with a 'quip' from his wonderful sense of fun and humour.

On this occasion there was no unexpected surprise in his summing up, when he said "Well, mum, it seems you're just like a Martini... any time, any place, anywhere."

I 'walked' straight into that one, I thought. Nevertheless a sense of humour is a gift too, as it no doubt lifts the spirit.

PROUD FEATHER

It is not known who told the first story about the 'receiving' of white feathers. White feathers are physical signs from the spiritual realms, from the Angels and those people we know, our loved ones in spirit .Throughout our spiritual history there have been many similar stories of the signs and symbols that have been presented to individuals in many shapes and forms, not necessarily as white feathers, as God, the Angels, and our loved ones will show you whatever sign they know you will and can relate to.

These signs and symbols are shown and given to us for a purpose. Its purpose is to give us spiritual comfort, a confirmation, and understanding. They are Angelic messages, like a calling card requesting an acknowledgement or a sign to an answer but most of all a sign and a seal of 'Faith'.

Sometimes such a delivery lays the foundations to opening up a belief system to someone who didn't have any. These white feathers are embraced as an absolute treasure by many believers and are often cherished as such.

There are stories of feathers arriving unexpectedly and at poignant times, but always with perfect timing. They are often found in very unusual places and for some people very little explanation is needed. A white feather is an 'acknowledgement' or an 'answer'. Generally, they are to be understood as a communication, whether this communication is from God, the Angelic realms, or our loved ones in spirit, leaving you to decide and confirm. They can act as someone's signature or an answer to a problem or just a confirmation to say that their loved one has reached the other side and all is well. They are never the less beautiful, comforting of psychical signs.

It can mean many things to different people but they are a communication nevertheless. Once we receive our first feather and it has made that connection in thought, it will become a part of our very own belief system. And usually, will be the beginning to receiving more. I personally have received a number of them in significant and unusual places and at poignant times, or both.

It has not been unusual that during someone's sitting a loved one in spirit has asked if the loved one here has received the white feather that they had sent.

Spirit has often pinpointed people to me, who have the 'white feather' belief.

I remember a young man in spirit asking his mother just this. He added that he had not only sent her one feather but a dozen or more, as she had kept them all. When I asked about the feathers, she squealed with delight.

She was given even more confirmation about her son's sent 'treasures'. She received an added bonus shortly after her sitting. It was as she was leaving my house, she found a feather on the path. She picked it up and looked at me, as if she found gold, as she boldly stated "it wasn't there when I arrived".

I just looked up at the sky and said a hearty "thank you." It was with ultimate perfect timing, I thought.

We will continue to receive them. Each will be attached to a separate thought or understanding, but still it is a 'solid' communication - an apport.

Ask and we will receive – belief is all it takes. I have met far too many people who have received a white feather and some have even a collection. Each white feather is responding to a thought of love that continues into the next world. One particular 'feather' experience I recal,l had a rather unusual 'edge' to it though.

It was whilst I was giving sittings to a group of young women. I instantly felt very drawn to one of them. I 'sensed' she had a brother in spirit whose name was Steve. I described him as being the life and soul of the party. He wanted to make her laugh and smile again. In fact he said he wanted to dance with her around the room. I 'sensed' he had a loud gregarious personality. It seemed she wanted to smile but I felt that she felt guilty somehow about doing so. People often do in grief.

I understood why she was reluctant to smile. There was the added trauma to his passing, it being such an horrendous case of murder.

It was then I was shown a series of 'visions' of the

circumstances in which he passed. I could see him lying on a concrete floor outside a building with a number of men kicking blows to his head. He mentioned London, as this was the place where it has all happened. I relayed all what I 'saw 'and told her just so. He was at peace and he knew he had got justice, as the men responsible for his murder was now serving time.

He wanted so much to take those horrific thoughts away from her. His wish was to be remembered as the 'happy-go-lucky' person he was, and for all the fun times that she'd had with him during his life. He didn't want her to dwell on the way he passed. He was communicating with the purpose of making her smile again.

I told her that she'd been playing his CD in her car, as he often sat beside her and swung his arms to the rhythm of the music. Something that he did in this life, and still does.

"Please, please. He wants you to smile, he wants you to laugh. He wants you to remember all the funny jokes he used to tell you."

He was so gregarious. I then had a vision of him dancing round the living room. I could hear music playing in my mind; this music was in sync with his movements. He was dancing to an Abba song. I told her just this.

"You can see him! Tell him I love him!" she cried.

"There is no need, he can hear you." I said.

Her face lit up. She laughed and cried as she gave confirmation about the dance routines that she and he used to do. She admitted she hadn't laughed in such a long time. She had listened to my running commentary of his antics until her facial expression turned to joy for just those moments. That was something he came to achieve with his presence, and he certainly did.

It was at the end of her sitting she said she had got something to show me and she wanted to know whether it was from him.

She went to another room and returned holding a box and handed it to me. I opened it and they're inside the box was a large white feather. I hadn't seen one so big.

"Is it from Steven?" she asked.

"Yes. I have no doubt it is, but it has something do with a birthday doesn't it?" I was prompted to ask.

She beamed and explained that it had arrived on her birthday for she had found it on the mat behind the front door, slotted between the birthday cards that had been posted that morning.

I was examining the feather as I was intrigued by the unusual sheer size of it. I lifted it from the box and held it up to the light. I noticed it wasn't exactly white.

"Look at this," I said "this feather isn't exactly white; it seems to have a slight pink tinge around the edge."

Then a thought came in from spirit.

"Was your brother Gay?" I asked.

"Yes," she gasped. "He was, and very proud of it." she laughed and cried.

"Well my goodness, to think the Gay people who have crossed over are now sending pink feathers and with great PRIDE too. How wonderful is that?"

We both smiled and laughed. Both clearly warmed by his 'presence' and his 'innovative' way of communicating.

It was a 'first' and I have no doubt it won't be the last, dear Steven and friends.

THE FAIRY GODMOTHER

A young pretty dark-haired woman named Michelle arrived at my door following a phone call from her desperate mother. Her mother had pleaded with me to see her daughter. She gave me no information regarding her situation other than the fact that Michelle was in a predicament and didn't seem to listen to any of her advice. She hoped I would give her more insight to her problems and maybe some hope for the future. Most of all, she hoped that she may start to listen to somebody, and maybe someone in spirit.

As soon as Michelle sat down to commence her sitting, I in my mind's ear could hear a lady in spirit, shouting, "You've got to leave him!"

The lady had a London accent. I 'sensed' it was Michelle's grandmother. The sitting had begun almost instantly.

"You have your grandmother in spirit, who was from London. She is telling me, 'You've just got to leave him.'"

I could hear her grandmother's anxious plea repeatedly. She was desperate to get her message across to her beloved granddaughter, referring to the abusive relationship that seemed to revolve around Michelle. This was the crux of the matter, which concerned not only

Michelle's mother but her Grandmother in spirit too.

Michelle's spirit was almost broken. I sensed her lack of self-esteem and her weariness. Her body language was draped in such a way it told me how 'ashamed' of being downtrodden she was. Her turmoil of emotions was connecting to my own psyche. Looking at her was like looking at me many years ago. She was in a state of not knowing what to do, who to talk to or where to go.

Michelle's response to her Grandmother's communication was not totally unexpected considering the state she was in. She seemed to believe she was wrapped up in a 'no hope' situation, that she could not see any end to. But her thought process was a result of what she was being told and led to believe by a controlling partner. Although she opened up about her situation, knowing that her loved ones in spirit knew what she was going through. It seemed the evidence of her Grandmother's communication did not have enough impact. But it was then I was given a 'vision', a glimpse of her future and words of hope. Michelle listened attentively as I told her I could see man in his thirties, who drove a van for a living. This was the man that was coming into her life and would change it for the better. I told her when she meets him; he will be going through a divorce at the time, I described his personality traits and gave her such detail, even down to a scar on his left hand.

She interrupted and seemed to dampen her message of hope.

"Who would want me with all my problems?" she asked. I understood this to be a typical response coming from an abused woman with low self-worth.

Then all of a sudden I had another 'vision' of a small boy with snow white hair. I continued to tell her that I could see her being happy enough in this future relationship, to have another child but this time it will be a little boy with snow white hair, a total contrast of the two dark skinned and dark haired boys she already had. This little boy was also there waiting to come, this child, I told her, would bring a lot love into her life.

She seemed to think that everything I had told her, sounded like the ending to a fairy tale. But she seemed lifted as she broke into a smile.

"Don't take this funny," she said, "But you sound like my fairy Godmother. If it all happens like you say it will, and I do meet my man and have that little boy, then you will have to be the Godmother. I promise you that."

She thanked me and asked if she could come to see me again soon as she said if anything, the sitting and I had made her feel so much better. She left knowing deep down what she had to do with her life, but when would she get enough courage to do it, was the big question. I felt she would do things in her 'own time' but not immediately. By this I mean, that everything really happens within God's perfect timing not Michelle's.

My thoughts were confirmed months later when she

came back for another sitting. Again this time another instant connection from the spirit of her Grandmother, which happened just as quickly as the last sitting.

"She's run back!" shouted her concerned Grandmother, indicating that Michelle had left her partner but had gone back again, repeating an old cycle of events that she still had to learn, somehow to break.

She was surprised again, that I and her Grandmother, knew instantly about her situation. She hung her head in response. So I spoke in depth about how spirit knows of our lives here and our troubles. I explained how we can obtain guidance and advice but also hope for the future as in this case.

I wasn't surprised to be shown once again, the man that would come on her path way to change things and the repeated 'vision' of the little boy with snow white hair, who was there still waiting it seems. I reassured her once again and reminded her that this life is about not how many problems we have, but it is how we deal with them that really counts. She needed the reassurance once again to lift her up, knowing there was help on the way, but she had to play a part in helping herself too.

In life we do what we physically can and leave the rest to God, the almighty Spirit and his 'helpers' of course. I knew it was only a matter in the process of time before the welcomed changes would occur.

A year or so later Michelle made another appointment

to see me. As I opened the door to greet he,r this time, she stood with a beaming smile on her face, holding and waving a piece of paper in her hand. I could sense a bright energy about her persona. Her aura was illumed. She couldn't get the news she wanted to tell me, out of her mouth, quick enough.

"I've met him! I've met him!" she said, as she waved the piece of paper under my nose.

"I had written all of what you told me down on a piece of paper, the last time we met. He's just as you described. He's in his thirties, he drives a van for a living, he's going through a divorce and his birthday is in February and oh my God, he has a scar on his left hand. I just can't believe it. He befriended me at first and made me look at my life, the total mess I found myself in. But really it's all thanks to you, of course."

"How wonderful," I said. "But you must thank your Grandmother too, and most of all God."

This time her sitting was mainly about giving confirmation of what had recently happened in her life and the moves and progress she had made, but still the 'vision' of the little boy with the snow white hair reappeared. Michelle went away with the comfort knowing that the relationship was going to a much deeper level and there was going to be another child for her, on the horizon for sure.

It was in a phone call from Michelle some months later that her faith in the newly found experience of the spirit world became a little doubtful, to say the least.

The tone in her voice was low, as she told me that she had become pregnant and that her and her new partner was delighted. She began to explain that a few weeks into the pregnancy she was rushed into hospital in excruciating pain, with an 'Ectopic 'pregnancy. This resulted in the removal of one of her fallopian tubes. I was saddened by the news.

"I doubt very much I'll ever have that little boy with the snow white hair now, I've got fifty per cent less chance of ever getting pregnant. Maybe the boy you saw was a boy I might have lost in a previous miscarriage as I've been told that miscarriages cross over and grow up on the other side." she said, giving me some glimpse of her new-found knowledge of the realms of spirit.

"Can my pathway change?" she asked.

"No, not really. It's mapped out from day one." I replied.

But I told her I had no doubts about what I had seen in the previous sitting with regards to the little boy with snow-white hair, that was waiting to arrive here. Although this time I wasn't having a vision as I spoke to her. I knew what I had seen and felt before. I told her not to give up and not be too disheartened and to think of the positives in her life. She was in a much better position than she was back then.

"Just wait and see... Let things unfold." I said

I did my very best to reassure her. I began to question myself a little. I am only a mere mortal after all. But I was concrete sure of what I 'saw'. The answer finally came twelve months or so later.

Michelle gave birth to a little boy with snow white hair. He was the 'glimpse' of hope that was to be Michelle's future, she named him Ciann.

Michelle's new partner was Catholic, something that Michelle wasn't, as she did not belong to any particular denomination, although she held some personal beliefs that she had revered in recently.

It so happened that to enable Ciann to become baptized, Michelle had to be baptized too. So to my surprise in the process, I was asked to become her Godmother, something she had joked about at her first sitting. Perhaps it was Michelle having her own insight on things back then. I was quite honoured with my Godmother status. In fact she now insists on calling me her 'Fairy Godmother' at the start of each of her unmistakable phone calls.

Michelle's story is about gaining advice and obtaining insight from the realms of spirit to enable us enact change but most of all a lesson about not giving up on the hope that is sometimes shown to us. Never doubting or worrying especially when the odds are against us, even when there seems to be very little hope left. Do not give up. The answers to our problems eventually resolve, if not immediately and maybe not in the way we assume or expect

Michelle & Cian

but what God 'lays out' before us, is meant to be, regardless.

    We are given 'insight' to certain things along our journey. Some things we need to know. It is those certain things that will truly be of benefit to us, while some things are best left unsaid. Insight can be shown to us to protect us from an added anxiety or sorrow and, as for most things on our journey, this is best to be left to unfold naturally. Life is a process of inevitable and unexpected changes.

WISDOM

Having given this 'knowledge' it will enable us to understand the process of our journey and enable us to shield ourselves and sometimes make triumph over our situations.

If it were the case that we could obtain all the answers to our problems though a 'channel', we would be living a perfect life, without the nurture of spiritual growth. This journey is not about 'perfection'.

Spiritual growth comes from enduring tasks, which is part of our journey here, on earth. These 'Lessons' and 'tests' in life will help the development of our soul, and aid the understanding of ourselves as the spiritual beings, that we truly are.

CALL OF DUTY

Wouldn't it be wonderful if I could answer every request and 'solve' every mystery or criminal case that came to my attention?

There are those you can help and those you clearly can't, and it is the ability to distinguish between the two that is a true 'gift' of wisdom. There are always insights but sometimes there is no resolution and it is in those cases a mystery will remain and become the pain in someone's journey, someone's life lesson.

There are certain cases I have had to give very careful consideration to. There are times when I have to give special thought to my own ethics, morals, and principles. Sometimes even consider a country's 'political persuasion'. Not to mention the importance of my own personal safety issues.

In the past I have 'walked' into cases blind to the potential consequences, where I've been told by the person who had initially instigated my involvement, 'not to worry, as I would be well protected'. It was then I realized the seriousness of possible consequences involved.

I remember one case where I didn't need to use my psyche or any other of my gifts to be made aware. My common sense told me not to get involved, without breaking confidentiality.

I received an email during the Christmas period, marked 'Highly Confidential'. I almost dismissed it as junk mail, but the subtitle caught my attention; 'Humanitarian Criminal Investigation'.

I opened the email only to find It was a genuine request from a Chief Detective in Peru that was working with an organisation, a humanitarian group, who were fighting a war against the 'trafficking' of women and children. I was asked to use my 'insights' for number of purposes relating to certain peoples disappearances and a number of recovered bodies.

Attached to the e-mail were very graphic photographs of the 'innocents' killed in the process of unlawful killings, which were a result of the organised crime, which seems to rule certain cities and towns. I was sickened by what I saw. I felt a sense of helplessness and fear at the same time.

Nonetheless, I had to withdraw from this request and contain the response to my feelings. It certainly struck 'cords' within me. It made me and think about the horror and injustice involved. It taught me an 'awareness' I can never forget. It left me feeling somewhat humbled and honoured, to be asked to become involved in such important cases. But considering all the potential consequences, a line had to be drawn.

THE LITTLE PEBBLE

Phone calls, letters and e-mails continue to arrive daily from the 'little pockets' all over the world wanting pieces of me and my 'Gifts'. There are those requests that are complicated and strange, even funny sometimes. Some requests that have to be questioned and even refused. Although I do endeavour to help people, spiritually, wherever and whenever possible.

It was January 2007, during a busy morning when I was ploughing through my emails that I noticed one with the subject heading 'Greetings from Australia'.

It was worded in an informal and cheerful manner. I was half expecting it be a response from a TV viewer.

I was surprised to find it was from a Bishop named Malcolm Broussard. He said he was a Catholic Bishop and the Spiritual Director of a Catholic 'seer' named William Kamm, who was presently serving Sentence, in the Goulburn Correctional Centre in New South Wales, Australia. He told me William Kamm was known around the world as 'The Little Pebble'.

Bishop Malcolm Broussard said William Kamm was wrongfully convicted of a crime he did not commit and his legal team had put in an appeal against this conviction. He also told me that he was following instructions from William Kamm, who wanted him, to make contact with me.

There were important questions he wanted to ask me. He wanted to know, 'When will William Kamm be released from prison? When would he be fully vindicated?' He wanted me to ask this through 'Our Lord and his holy Angels' for the consolation of The 'Little Pebble'.

Bishop Malcolm Broussard said he could reassure me that William Kamm was an innocent man.

I must admit I hadn't heard of 'The Little Pebble' but did experience 'gut feelings' when I read the content of this email.

I thought about it for a while. I thought about the whole concept, and a number of things sprang to mind. I imagined that the only way he knew of me was through my book, *Angela's Angels,* or my TV episode of *Psychic Investigators* that had been shown on the Australian ABC TV channel in December, weeks earlier.

My mind boggled, I felt I needed to research the names in question and this case which seemed so unreal.

Knowing the Catholic Church as I did, something didn't seem quite right. I thought about the details, then the whole concept. That a prisoner, a 'man of the cloth', so I was being told, was sitting on the other side of the world in his prison cell, had heard about me and my works and decides to turn to me just seemed so surprising .

It was with these doubts that I had to gather all my 'faith' and make a plea for assistance in finding some answers.

Perhaps he did become aware of me through my book *Angela's Angels*, I thought to myself. He would not be the first member of the 'clergy' to have told me that they had read my book.

Maybe his 'Bishop' was in doubt about this man's innocence and was asking for his own purpose. I really was baffled but I still held on to my initial gut reaction and thoughts.

Nevertheless, I decided to keep the email. I filed it and planned to return to it later with more scrutiny.

But it was half an hour later I received another email from the same Bishop. This time, he had said he'd received more mail from William Kamm asking him once again to contact me, and asking more questions about whether there was a 'conspiracy' surrounding his conviction.

Bishop Malcolm Broussard said that William Kamm had told him that he was aware that I helped to solve crimes through the intercession of God's Angels.

It was at that point, I couldn't hold on to my curiosity

any longer. I decided I had to look on the Internet for any press coverage on this case.

As it turned out, the case of 'The Little Pebble' was one of Australia's biggest cases ever. William Kamm, the world renowned 'Little Pebble' was originally a Catholic priest who had been extradited from the Catholic Church.

He was a 'self-proclaimed seer'. He was found to be a cult leader, who had established his own variation of Catholicism by establishing his own 'Church', which became a 'shield' to abuse children and consequently he was charged and had been found guilty of sexual abuse of children.

The survivors of child sexual abuse are something I hold close to my heart. I had worked in Child Protection for many years, and have been a witness to far too many soul-destroying cases of this type. As I read more about the case, I found my stomach churning just like it used to.

Unfortunately back then in Social Services, during those case procedures my thoughts, feelings and insights could understandably not be recorded. I would have to keep them close to my chest or only share them 'off the record' with the 'believers' amongst my work colleagues but in hindsight I was nearly never wrong.

In this instance, my gut reaction about the email was right too. I had instantly felt that there was something sinister about the email request. I knew that the appeal would fail and that he would continue to serve his sentence.

Besides, if this man really was a 'seer' he should be able to 'receive' his own answers, I thought.

This was another one of the times that it felt 'right' not to reply to these emails, for obvious reasons. I did keep them and filed them all the same, as I thought maybe they would be of interest sometime in the future. I have a habit of collating items and articles of 'spiritual evidence'. They are often reminders of how diverse, my work can be and sometimes how strange coincidences and synchronicities constantly present themselves before me.

One such time was Four years later, I was being interviewed by a Journalist from a National newspaper. I was asked whether I had received any strange requests over the years, or if there were any cases I would not get involved in and where would I draw the line.

The case of 'The Little Pebble' came to mind immediately and I let slip about the emails I had received from the Bishop years earlier.

The journalist thought it would make a great piece of news, as they always look for 'sensationalism' in their news stories. She saw the story as something parallel to me receiving letters from 'Jack the Ripper', as she must have been aware of the Australian public's hatred towards this man.

The story became headline news in the Herald Sun, Australia's biggest national Sunday paper. The headline read: 'RELIGIOUS SEX FIEND ASKS FOR PSYCHIC'S AID'.

One of my philosophies in life is that something good always comes out of something bad. It was from the exposure I got through that article, that I was able to help many more people from Australia via telephone. I had a spate of new 'Aussie' callers requesting even more answers from myself and 'my Angels.'

HEAVEN'S PENSION

Two young women sat before me. They introduced themselves as sisters Mary and Jane. They seemed to wriggle about in their seats nervously in anticipation as they waited to see what their loved ones in spirit had to say.

I heard a gentleman's voice from spirit say

"That's my daughter."

I felt drawn to look at Jane. I was puzzled as I heard it over again and again.

I felt drawn, once more, and I found myself saying to her. "Jane, you have a father in spirit."

They both looked at each other.

"Me?" she said, looking baffled, pointing to herself.

I heard the voice again, I was still feeling compelled to look at Jane.

"That's my daughter." I heard the voice say bluntly, and it wasn't said in the plural sense of the word. It was then I realised they must be half-sisters.

"You're actually half-sisters, aren't you?" I asked.

"How did you know that?" Jane piped up. "I'm sorry; I forgot to tell you we were. But I don't think my dad's in spirit, though. But there again, I haven't seen him for nearly seven years, so really I wouldn't know. Are you sure it's my Dad and not my Granddad, Angela?" she asked, bemused.

I too, was shocked, as my policy is never to give messages of death or bad news. I reached out for her hand and looked into her eyes and started to relay the words her father wanted her to hear.

"Please, listen to what I have to say," I said, the vibration was strong. "I know this must be in a terrible shock for you and I apologise profusely if I'm wrong. But by the sounds of it, this gentleman is in the spirit world, and he is adamant that you're his daughter. Please listen to what he has to say. He wants to say he's sorry to you and your mother, he's sorry for the way he treated your mother and sorry for the amount of money he wasted." I continued….

"He was what you would call a 'real charmer' but I sensed that his drink problem, had got the better of him. The whole essence of his spirit told me that he was a bit of a 'ladies' man' too.

I could hear more of his words. "Wine, women and song, that was me." he said as he summed up his actions in this life.

I looked at Jane. Jane was looking aghast.

"You were his little girl, so he says." I added.

Jane looked with me with melting eyes, as I felt an

abundance of regret from both sides.

"There is a lot of love being sent to you. Your dad wants forgiveness for not being the father he should have been and most of all forgiveness from your mother for spending all her well earned money and for leaving her penniless too."

Jane had listened intently. She sat taking sharp intakes of breath with each statement and sentence.

"My God, you've got him to a tee." she said.

"It's Ron." I said as I heard him shout his name.

She was totally speechless and motionless, in a mild state of shock. I think she needed to hear things again. Jane was quiet for a while as the thoughts, that had transcended from spirit swirled around in her head. I suppose she couldn't completely grasp things at that moment.

"This is unbelievable…" she muttered. Apparently she'd never had a sitting before and didn't know what to expect. I explained even more about how spirit communicates.

When she finally stood up to leave. She asked if she could have another sitting soon and this time could she bring her mother Vera along. I openly invited both of them. It was some weeks later before I could schedule another sitting but soon enough Jane and her mother Vera arrived.

I had remembered the initial possible discrepancy over

the issue of whether her father was actually in spirit or still alive. Vera sat on the edge of her seat waiting for an appropriate moment to say something, I felt. I had geared the conversation and sort of dismissed her eagerness to a talk, as I was far too eager to start the sitting, in hope that spirit would re-address and rectify the issue once more.

Vera ,quickly, reminded me of what I had said, but I had to stop her in her tracks, as undeniably, Ron came and communicated a second time. This time he communicated personal memories for Vera and again there were apologies for his behavior and what he called his unforgivable actions.

Vera nodded and agreed. Vera seemed an easy going lady, very unassuming. She didn't appear angry with him, I felt she must of have loved him dearly and still did.

"Oh well, that's life isn't it? We love and we live, and we live and we learn." said Vera.

She was quite a philosophical lady, I thought. There seemed to be no bitterness or her part.

"Oh Angela," she continued to say. "I've been dying to tell you. You were and are so right about everything. When my daughter came home from her sitting with you and told me about her father, I approached the Registrar's Office almost straight away and within four days I was holding his Death certificate. He'd actually died two years ago. I know this sounds strange, but I can't thank you enough, as you have done me the greatest favour. You see Ron left me penniless and went off with another woman, but he never actually divorced me. This means I can now claim widow's pension, which is a little more than what I'm getting now but I found out since I can have it backdated two years, it seems." she laughed a little and cried at the same time.

Bless Ron, I thought. This was his way of 'returning' some of her money he had wasted.

"It's not me you need to thank, it's Ron. He obviously had some unfinished business to do and don't forget he wants your forgiveness too."

She looked up towards the heavens and in a finesse sort of a way and said;

"'Thank you, Ron, God bless you."

I had no doubts that Ron was not only granted the blessing to communicate. But it also seemed he made the most of his short time. It allowed him to make amends in more ways than one and it seems that he can now rest in peace in true 'loving' memory.

SPIRIT UNION

The 'sisters' visit triggered a similar memory from a few years before, when another unsuspecting couple named Gary and Lynne came to visit me. They sat snuggled up close, holding hands with each other. I sensed an air of secrecy about them, and that they had come with some sort of an agenda on their minds. They confirmed this by stating that the purpose of their visit was to find out something, not necessarily just to receive communication from a loved one.

People do come to me for answers of many kinds but when the request is a statement as blunt and direct as that, I cannot say it didn't make me feel a little apprehensive. However, I must always remind myself that the power of Spirit never ceases to fail.or amaze me. It became obvious from meeting them, that their understanding of the process in which I work was not clear. I reminded them that all the information that I 'receive' comes from the Realms of Spirit, whether it is from my Guides or their loved ones or both, but fundamentally it stems from a profound belief in God. This sitting seemed to warrant a few words beforehand.

I began.

"Now then, just sit and relax for a few moments. I want you to send loving thoughts to everyone you know in spirit. Don't concentrate on any one person, for if you do, you will be closing your mind down. Believe wholeheartedly for the time that we share together that there is a spirit world and our loved ones can communicate and they will. We ask this through the power of God, we ask for his words of comfort and hope, and that we ask in his name. Amen."

Linda and Gary just looked at one another and smiled gently.

Linda broke the silence, as she started to scurry about in her handbag and handed me a watch.

"I understand you can 'feel' things from objects. This might help you, as we need to know something." she said.

As soon as the watch touched my hand. I sensed the 'energy' of who it once belonged to, as I looked up at Lynne. I told her that it was her father's watch.

But Lynne showed no expression, as if to not give anything away. Within a few seconds, I heard a man's voice.

I looked at Gary and told him it was his father's watch too. The 'couple' that had sat before me, weren't actually a 'couple' as such, like they had first portrayed and which I had assumed.

"You're brother and sister, aren't you?" I asked.

"Well yes, we are." said Gary. They looked at one another. "Can you tell me more? Are you sure this man was father to me and Lynne?"

I was 'instrumented' to look at Lynne as I heard the gentleman's voice again say he was her father and Gary's too.

A picture started materializing in my mind. I could see a tall man with dark wavy hair plastered with Brylcreem. I was then 'shown' a shop, a General Stores which seemed to be situated in a small rural village. Both had a connection with the father I was 'seeing'.

I described what I had 'seen' to Gary and Lynne. They both answered 'yes' in unison but there were no other words of confirmation. I felt that they were trying to build up to a point of telling me something but held back for the 'right' moment. Their real agenda I had no doubt was that they were determined to test the Spirit World. I sensed there was something that had to be crystal clear.

"I've just heard the name Derek." I said.

"Yes!" they both seemed to shouted together in unison.

It was then Lynne reached again into her handbag and pulled out an envelope which appeared to contain a number of photographs.

She wanted to conclude something at that point.

"Right then, if this man that you see, named Derek, yeah? You're saying that he is my father and Gary's father also. Would you mind so much if I showed you these photographs?" She said', as she laid the photographs in front of me. All were black and white photos; many seemed to be taken in the 1950's-60's, it appeared. I noticed they were all of different men, some taken in groups, weddings, outings, family gatherings and there were some of individuals.

"Now then is the man that you are 'seeing', is he in any of these photographs?"

I glanced down and spotted Derek, my hand automatically pointed straight to the photograph.

"Look, this is the man I see, this is your father."

They both smiled, and squeezed each other's hand. I noticed Gary wink at Lynne. Gary's eyes became glazed.

"Without sounding rude... I said.... "now that we've established what he really looks like, I feel he needs to say something."

I felt his presence. He seemed to want to say more. I heard his words in my mind as I gathered them together.

"What Auntie said is true...what Auntie said is TRUE!." I

repeated his words.

With that remark they both squealed with delight, as they flung their arms around each other and wept.

I looked on, open mouthed. I'd never seen such a reaction during a sitting, they looked so surprised and after being somewhat confused. I knew I must have hit the nail on the head, whatever it meant. Gary interrupted their excitement to explain what the last comment meant.

"What you're saying Angela means so much to us, and I suppose, to Lynne most of all. I was always told that Lynne was adopted but have always felt that Lynne was more than an adoptive sister; as there has been a real bond between us and Lynn has felt the same.

It was only after my father Derek died, we were told by an Aunt, that Lynne was a result of an affair that my Father Derek had, had. Unfortunately Lynn's mother, my father's lover, died in childbirth, giving birth to Lynne.

At the time, my father and my mother, God rest her soul - who must have been an all-forgiving – woman, they decided to introduce Lynne into the family as an adoptive child. I remember my older brothers and sisters weren't too happy at the time. But I always seemed to sense that there was a real bond, a natural bond between us.

Lynne and I have always been so close. Now by what you've said, it all makes so much sense and confirms and seals the whole matter. So my 'father's skeleton' finally came out the 'closet', she is truly my half- sister. We'd heard recently that other people suspected it, but dismissed it as being just a 'rumour'.

It wasn't until my Father's Sister told us the 'family secret' just after my father's funeral, as she felt that Lynne needed to know who her real father was. My other brothers and sisters would not accept it. Both Lynne and I always felt that there was something there. The only way we could follow up what my Auntie said for sur, was from my father himself, or shall I say my father's spirit and through someone like you, of course."

He said he couldn't thank me enough. Gary and Lynne both reached out and hugged me almost simultaneously. I must admit my eyes filled with tears too.

Lynne and Gary sat hugging one another, crying, knowing that their questions had been answered. These were answers they had longed for during most of their lives. They were not only reunited with their father's spirit but they two, were truly, without a question, UNITED by Spirit alone.

SEEKING JUSTICE

People don't only seek and receive words of comfort from loved ones in spirit, who will often speak of fond memories of their lives they once shared. There are people who come to me seeking truth and justice. They may want to find out the truth surrounding a loved one's passing or guidance to enable them to seek more 'truths' and justice. Sometimes their loved one in spirit will let them know they are aware that they are still seeking truth and justice on their behalf, and this 'knowledge' of the justice being sought is often shared. The powerful feeling of loss coupled with the emotion surrounding injustice must be the greatest pain of all.

Many an answer has been given through spirit communication. It is nothing unusual for people to approach me in the initial stages or half way through court procedures, as the angst of waiting for an outcome becomes too unbearable as their need to know the outcome of the case to settle down the severity of their anxieties and severe emotions. They come to me in hope of peace of mind.

As we know, sometimes the 'scales' of legal system can be imbalanced and morally wrong. Meeting with such people who have experienced loss, coupled with injustice is soul- destroying to say the least.

Injustice seems to stir up an emotion in me that touches the core of my being, my soul. It makes me want to put things 'right' if I can. However, if an injustice can't be reversed, so be it. I have to be humble and come to terms with I, as I am only a' hopeful messenger', a channel.

Sometimes those 'truths' that are given can be difficult to accept, and become part of the pain we must bear. For pain is part of our journey here on the earth plane. It is part of our spiritual growth and development.

To suffer emotional pain is inevitable, nobody escapes that lesson. Life can be unjust but it is our faith, the belief in the unseen, which give us some kind of balance we need to survive.

Our faith helps us to achieve great things; anything is possible if you believe in the power of God. We can gain truth and strength, justice and peace from spirit. I was always told that justice comes from God's right Hand and that, I have been a 'witness' to.

MARTIN

Pamela Green was such a lady who was suffering injustice.

It was after she had read a newspaper article about my recent guest appearance at her local town's bookstore. I had been doing a book signing in Burton on Trent in Derbyshire. I did not know at the time that an article of Pamela's plight and a photo of her son, made front page news, of the same paper which had wrote an article about my visit.

When she phoned to make an arrangement for a sitting, she mentioned that she felt very drawn to me as the location where my photograph had been taken, had great significance to her and a loved one. We arranged to meet a couple of weeks later.

Her loved one was Martin, her son. He communicated his name; I seemed to grasp it immediately as we sat down together.

Martin told me he was her only son. He mentioned a 'troubled' life caused by his addictions. But most of all he wanted to send love to his mother and his children. He mentioned something about his mother's struggle; I sensed it was an immense Legal struggle. Martin wanted Justice, so he said. He knew his mother had a massive battle on her hands. He 'told' his mother not to give up. Martin said he often drew close to her, to give her strength, as he knew her spirit was low. Pamela was going through a roller-coaster of emotions on a daily basis.

Martin seemed adamant with the sheer force of his words he wanted ' Justice' as he kept repeating the words loud and clear. He 'mentioned' the European Court of Justice, confirmed by a picture which flashed up in my mind. He knew that the 'Justice' campaign continued to struggle and was 'falling on 'deaf ears'. Pamela confirmed everything. It was unmistakably all true.

She then told me the crux of her heartache and the reason for her campaign. Martin had died of dehydration eleven days after of being admitted to Prison. She understood that he died through neglect, due to lack of care and procedures. You didn't have to a Medium to detect the injustice here. Martin's plight was another such case that touched the core of my being.

Pamela seemed alone, only armed with a mother's love and God's righteousness on her side, to take on the enormity of a battle against the Government.

She told me she had a meeting coming up with Jack Straw, the Home Office Minister, that week in hope to draw further attention to Martin's case. But most of all she needed to know that Martin was aware of what was happening and to know that she was trying her very best to get Justice.

Martin was so, obviously aware of her dilemma and the seemingly endless battle, as it had been going on for a number of years and understandably would continue to do so. But I 'knew' and Martin 'knew' that the might of her spirit and courage, coupled with her son's love, and with the power of prayer, It would see her through to the very end. but not until Government- run prisons refrain from being immune to prosecution. Sometimes what is legally right can be so morally wrong. Justice in the eyes of God can and will be done. Until then, God Bless them.

Martin Green

BUSTER

It was a day when I was absorbed with the usual mundane tasks. I was out shopping around the small village where I live. Such simple tasks keep me earthbound in my thoughts. I welcome the mundane things as they can be a relief from the spiritual aspect of my nature, as much as I am passionate about my work. The seriousness of spiritual work load, makes me appreciate those mundane tasks even more sometimes.

Panic set in, when I realized I had to dash back home. I was expected to do a telephone reading for a lady from London named Michelle, whose son, she was hoping to receive communication from. She had sent me his photograph in hope that I could hold on to it and 'receive'.

I wasn't aware of anything other than the fact she had a son in spirit. I was in a dilemma whether to cancel the appointment, as I wanted the conditions to be right. I felt I wouldn't have time to prepare myself properly. Ideally I like to be in that relaxed, calm, meditative mode in order to attune myself.

I just had enough time to grab the photograph when the phone rang. It was Michelle. I looked down at the photograph and looked into his eyes, 'the windows of his soul'. I instantly felt an overwhelming feeling of presence around me. There was no need to cancel the telephone sitting, as my 'psyche' was telling me not to. I quickly explained to Michelle the way I was feeling and I asked her politely to just listen to what I had to say. I needed that total peace and quiet for a while.

I started to receive 'visions' of the events which had led to the death of her son. I began to describe what I could 'see' through the eyes of his spirit, as he drew so close. It was like watching a film' a series of events which reeled off in my mind's eye.

He was stood on a corner of a street, outside a row of shops. I could see a gang of youths surrounding him, one of them was a young female.

I 'felt' a blow to his head and I wanted to hold my neck. I began to sense his feelings. He had been hit and stabbed.

I 'saw' him running down a road close by to the shops. He was running for home, holding the wound in his neck. He didn't make it home as he collapsed and died in the street. Michelle was there at those last moments. I began to sense Michelle's silent tears down the phone line. There was a silence and a long pause.

Michelle response, confirmed that's what had exactly happened. There was no mistake that this was her son who was communicating, as these were the last moments of his earthly life.

Then I felt the rush of emotion, an immense feeling of love he wanted to send to his mother.

"He wants to send you so much love Michelle," I said. I was now beginning to catch on to his words.

"There was someone involved in his murder with a Greek sounding name, which sounds like Sta-vos," I said as I tried to break the words down. I couldn't quiet grasp it. "The culprits have been found and charged." I added

"Yes that right. Stelios is the name, he's one that stabbed him and he is the only one that has been charged with his murder." she replied.

"I sense that the weapon was not found and was thrown into water." I continued.

"That's right, the knife was never found but the river Thames is close by and many suspect that that's where they got rid of it." Michelle replied.

"Your son mentions something about another case. What's this?" I said, slightly confused.

"That's what I wanted him to know. I wasn't happy with the so called 'justice'. I wanted the boy who struck him first charged too. As you mentioned he'd been struck on the head. So I am hoping to open up another case and bring the boy who did that to him to justice."

She gained some comfort knowing that her son knew of her intentions. It seemed to be the paramount reason for her call. I sensed she was already a strong believer in the afterlife.

Her son didn't want her to dwell on those last moments. I began to sense the traits of his personality, as his charm and charisma became apparent.

"Oh he's such a lovely charming, funny young man. He was very popular, I believe. He's talking about his girlfriends he had, more girlfriends than 'mates', so he tells me!" I said. I felt Michelle's spirit lift a little.

"He could be quite comical too!" I stated. Michelle agreed.

"He wants to remind you of the comical impressions he did of that popular comedian *Ali G*. Something he had to a 'tee', so I believe."

He was trying his best to lift his mother's spirit with happier memories.

"Talking of girls, he mentions his sisters and he wants to send love to them too."

"Yes, he has sisters. They miss him so much." came the reply.

"He used to 'torment' them in a fun, loving way." I added.

I told her that he comes and visits them too, and is very much around them. "He's talking of a nickname he had. I sense he's had it since he was a little toddler" I added.

"Yes that's right!" she replied. "His nickname was 'Buster' but his real name was Julian. His full name is Julian 'Buster' Knight." she added with great pride.

I felt his energy beginning to fade. The 'heavenly telephone message' was coming to an end. Michelle went over all that had been said and thanked me.

I then asked her if she wouldn't mind if I could keep a copy of his photograph as a beautiful reminder of his wonderful communication, as I told her that one day I would like to write about him and have photographs of my cherished 'callers' and 'visitors' substantiate things even more, to which she agreed. It is important to let people know that he and all other souls live on, and those souls know our every endeavour. In this case it was the family's fight for more proceedings. Bless them all and most of all, God Bless you, Buster.

.

JULIAN 'BUSTER' KNIGHT

BAZ II

I had received an e-mail from a woman named Donna, who said she'd had a sitting with me a couple of years previously and asked if she could she book another sitting.

I was surprised when I was greeted by a gentleman with a Liverpool accent who introduced himself as Barry, as I was expecting Donna that day.

He explained that Donna was his partner and she had encouraged him to come and take her place.

He said he was rather sceptical as he had tried 'this sort of thing' before with other Mediums. From his tone I could tell that what he was saying, he had clearly not been impressed by others he had met.. Unfortunately, I hear of so many disappointed people in similar circumstances.

I got the feeling that for him, I was his 'last resort' in gaining some hope. I sensed his agonising need. As he sat down, I 'saw' the outlined figure of man and a woman standing together in spirit, beside him.

I began to tell him that his mother and father had crossed over, and that they were drawing very close to him at this moment in time.

It became clear there was now, the outline of three 'figures' standing beside him. Who were all obviously, closely connected.

I could see standing between his mother and father, a young man. I knew then, that this young man was the reason why Barry was 'searching'. It was his Son that he so needed to 'hear' from.

"There is a young man in spirit. I do believe he is your son. He appears to be in his twenties and has only recently passed to spirit."

"Yes, go on..." Barry urged

Barry began to sit up straight. I felt it was then when he began to realise that this time, something very 'real' seemed to be happening.

"He only just died in March." he added.

What flashed up in my mind next was a photograph of an old 'friend' of mine named Baz McKenna from Newcastle upon Tyne, whose spirit I first met when his parents asked me to help 'resolve' his last moments. Baz's spirit stole the hearts of many, who read his story, which was chronicled in the media and also in my last book. I felt there were similarities between these two young men in spirit. I told

Barry about my 'friend in spirit,' Baz McKenna and some of his plight.

"My son's name is Baz too." he exclaimed. "I'm Barry, he's known as Baz, but his full name is Barry Latta, the same as me." The 'connections' were confirmed.

It was no coincidence that I saw my old friend then, I thought. I began to have 'visions' of Barry's son's last moments. I described what I could 'see'; a busy road, a dual carriageway with a garage nearby. It was late at night when it happened but I sensed it happened here in the Midlands, not Liverpool. I relayed to Barry what I was receiving.

Barry nodded silently. He wanted to hear more.

It was then I 'sensed' the blows to his sons head, which I gestured many times. Barry's eyes filled with tears as he told me that his son was stabbed 14 times in his head. It was almost like a frenzied attack by someone out of control, but I felt that the culprit was very much aware of his actions. Why I thought that, I didn't know. I told Barry the man responsible was from a different culture too and an argument had broken out between them.

"You're right, he was Somalian." Barry replied.

"What's this about September? I feel your son is trying to say that he's going to be with you in September." Baz's voice echoed in my mind.

"The court case is in September and this man who

killed him is trying to plead Diminished Responsibility."

I paused and thought for a while and then it was one of those moments when I spoke very prophetically, clearly and slowly as I said, "Don't worry, he'll get fourteen years, and there will be talk of an Extradition Order."

"I do hope so!" Barry wept.

Barry's son, Baz, communicated something about November too. It seemed very important to him. He also mentioned something about a little girl. I relayed his son's 'thoughts' to him.

"Baz's girlfriend is due to have his baby in November."

"Well I have no doubt he will be there that day too."I

Barry wiped his eyes for a final time and then composed himself. He seemed to glance around the room and then at me and then told me he 'felt 'so at peace'. He stood up and shook my hand a lot tighter, than he did when he first arrived. He smiled and left.

I prayed that that peace would continue and he would remember that feeling of peace. The peace of knowing all is well with his son.

It was the very next morning I woke up with unexpected inspired thoughts, profound words, from my Spirit Guide Therese. She does not visit me often enough, but I know she is always there at the end of a prayer or a thought. I repeated her words to myself, until I found a pen and paper to write them down. The words were so beautiful. They were obviously given for a reason and the reason I thought was that, it would make a wonderful final line, to a chapter, or an ending of a book. The words poignantly fitted to events later, so it seemed and 'finally' had dual purpose too.

Later that day, I received another email from Donna, Barry's partner. This time she was describing the positive change in Barry since his visit. Stating that he no longer walked as if he had 'shackles' rounds his ankles and there was a glimpse of a glint back in his eyes, but most of all she thanked me for helping her, to get her 'Scouse' back. (Scouse- a unique cultural personality, slang terminology- of one who hails from Liverpool).It was then I remembered the words of my Spirit Guide, Therese and how relevant they seemed to Barry's experience: the words were 'True Mediumship gives flame to a flickering soul'.

Not only did Barry gain 'flame, to his flickering soul' but some solace, peace and words of Justice.

These prophetic 'words' of Justice unfolded in September. The man charged with his son's murder got a fourteen year Prison sentence and Extradition Order.

Baz Latta's story about getting 'answers' ended just like my 'friend' Baz (McKenna) - both their 'communications' were highlighted in the media. But fundamentally it was to let the world know, that they have 'lived' on and could continue to communicate. God bless you both, my friends.

'BAZ' LATTA

KEILYN

It was on hot summer's day that a young handsome dark skinned man arrived at my door wearing a football kit. I assumed he had a connection with my son, who was a footballer. I was surprised when he said he had booked a sitting with me, as he barely looked old enough. His skin shone 'ageless 'in the brightness of the sunny day. He reassured me that he had booked a sitting and his name was Darren. I was even more surprised with what spirit had in stall.

He made himself comfortable on my sofa. I seemed to glance over his shoulder as I vividly 'saw' a small boy standing behind him. The boy's presence was so visual and so clear.

"I can see a beautiful looking little boy with you; he's about seven years old."

"Oh yes?" he said quite bluntly.

"He looks a lot like you," I continued.

"I sensed he went in very tragic circumstances, an accident."

"Yes." came the reply. Darren's eyes glistened as he began to look pensive. I could hear the little boy tell me that this young man was his Daddy.

"You don't look old enough to have a son of seven!" I remarked.

"People often tell me that. I suppose I do look young for my age. And yes I do have a son who's that age, who passed away. Can you actually see him?" he asked surprised.

I told him that I could see his son. Once again I had to put my full trust in spirit and just relay exactly what I could see and hear of his beautiful boy. I felt Darren's unconventional dress must have been a ploy, trying to throw me. But it was his son's presence that was so overwhelmingly powerful that cast away any doubts. It is known from my experience that children and young people of the spirit world often do communicate with such a powerful 'energy'. The young boy was pointing to a cross that hung around his neck, which I described.

His father then pulled down the neck of his football shirt he was wearing and showed me the exact same cross and told me that his son was laid to rest with one of the same.

Darren asked again, "You can actually see him? Tell me, what does he looks like then?"

For people who are relatively new to exploring the concept of the Afterlife, these sorts of questions are common.

"Well, his skin is lighter than yours, his hair is short and there's a tramline design through it. He has a beaming smile with beautiful dimples, and he is wearing a suit. He's dressed as if he's going to a wedding. He looks so smart and so handsome."

Darren was clearly moved by my description. His eyes glanced downwards, deep in thought. You could see the 'reality' of the 'vision' and what I was saying, was having an effect on him and on myself too. It's hard not to show emotions at times but as always spirit seems to keep me braced up on a high vibration until the communication is over and that is often when I feel it the most.

In this sitting, I felt I was being carried by the boy's energy. He was so vibrant and so eager to communicate; I began to feel a strong sense of familiarity between us. I felt connected once again in some way. I dismissed those feelings as I continued to hear what the young boy had to say.

I heard the little boy say something about his 'brothers'. This threw me a little. This 'young boy' had a number of siblings which surprised me even more. I mentioned that he was calling for his brothers. Darren confirmed that he was actually a father of four boys.

"Your little boy is saying something about the older one

and the playground."

I repeated this over and over again as his father searched his mind for an explanation.

"That's strange," he said "I have been called in to my boy's school, only this week, by my eldest son's teacher. She said she was concerned about him, as he had told her he could see his little 'brother' still playing in the playground. The teacher said that she put it down to the fact that he was grieving and suggested that some counseling would be appropriate to his needs."

I told Darren I had no doubt that his son in spirit wanted to play with his brother again and still does, but most of all to give him comfort, to let his family know that he is close and he still plays and visits you and the family.

"You can tell the teacher from me... he was there." I said without trying to sound obnoxious.

I then shared with him, some of my own memories of playing with spirit children, in my early school days, and that it wasn't uncommon particularly with sensitive children, which I sensed his older son was. I had no doubt about it.

The young boy's spirit continued to stand behind the sofa alongside his father, he seemed patient with me. He just stood there smiling.

I gave his father more explanation and understanding of spirit and the process of communication. There often is the need to, particularly for those who have recently been bereaved and are new to the process of Greif and Loss.

Often whilst I take time to do this. The spirit will wait patiently for interim periods for the knowledge from my Guides to be passed on. They are often influencing the sitting too, for it is important for the new sitter to understand this process. In turn, the little boy began to communicate once more. I could hear him mention someone called Kevin.

"Who's Kevin?"…..

"That's his best friend." his father confirmed.

"What's this about the sweets? He's saying thank you for the sweets."

"I've recently been told that Kevin, his best friend had gone to visit his grave this week, for the very first time. He had bought him a packet of sweets which he placed on his grave."

Then came a crucial moment.

"My son isn't giving you his name, is he?" Darren asked desperately.

I gathered this is what he needed to know so there would be no doubt at all in his mind that his son was with him there, standing in my living room beside him.

"I can only give you what I receive. I understand your

need but you never know." I replied.

Just then my head turned to the side. I found myself drawn, instrumented to look at a framed photograph, which I have on display of my 'adoptive' Goddaughter's son, Cian. The boy renowned as the 'Boy with the snow-white hair'.

"Your son has just said something like, this boy's name here," I said pointing to the photograph.

"This boy in the photograph is named Cian. It may not be that, but I feel that it is just as unusual." I then broke the sound of the name down to the two syllables "Ci-an, Ci-an…" I repeated.

Those sounds struck a major cord by the look on his father's face. He just crumbled and broke down in floods of tears.

"It's Keilyn, it's Keilyn," he repeated, as swallowed away the lump in his throat "That's what he is trying to say. His name is Keilyn. Keilyn, that's my boy… My God!" he cried.

The full force of Keilyn's presence and communication seemed to hit. The shock must have given him a bag of mixed emotions and thoughts as the communication seemed to becoming almost a complete 'reality' for him. Darren then had a surprise in store for me.

"I have something to tell you. You mentioned that my son went in a tragic accident. It was shortly after his accident that my partner who's not Keilyn's natural mother, came to visit you for a sitting last year. He came through then, as you described him to her as well and told her that he been involved in a 'hit and run' incident. You 'knew' that it had only recently happened. You also said that the person responsible had not been found. You told her to pass on a message to his family, which was that the person responsible was a local man and that he would be found. But sadly, the family would get very little justice. All what you said came true. They caught him, he did live locally. He was ordered to serve a 2 year sentence but after an appeal, he served only fourteen weeks in prison. No justice, no justice at all. When my partner came back from the sitting with you, I found it hard to believe. I thought she was trying to make me feel a little better as she knew I'd visited a 'so called' medium, days after Keilyn died, and that experience was just terrible. It just added insult to injury. I wore my football kit back then, I suppose I wanted to test him too. I apologize, by the way. I hope you understand. He seemed to conjure up generalized statements and mentioned stereotypical things, which related to my colour. He told me nothing about my son, in the end I told him straight. I demanded my money back and I walked out in disgust. So you see it's took me a long time to have the courage to come here, I had been so disheartened and I'm so glad I came now."

Keilyn was stood there still, and listened to every word. The spirit world had clearly embraced his Daddy, who was now truly open to the concept of an Afterlife. It was at this crucial stage that Keilyn wanted to tell him more.

"Tell him to stop, tell him to stop!" I could hear Keilyn shout. I knew he was referring to his daddy's tears. But Darren needed to continue to talk.

"Keilyn got killed outside his home. He died in my arms. I have been over those last moments time and time again. Why...why?" he asked almost pleading for an answer. His head sunk down and his tears continued to fall.

I heard Keilyn beg for his Daddy to stop crying. I placed my hand on his shoulder and told him that there was nothing he could have done to stop it from happening. I explained that I meet so many people who have lost loved ones, who think that in some way they could have changed events to prevent a loved one's passing by doing or saying something.

"There is nothing you or anyone could have done," I told him. "We are all born on a journey and we are all allocated a certain amount of time here. The way in which we pass whether naturally, accidentally or tragically is the way it was meant to be. Every second is mapped out. It really is meant to be, as 'Loss' is our greatest lesson. Forgive me, if you may not fully understand this belief. Keilyn was a highly evolved soul, these souls are often 'old headed' characters born with a certain amount of wisdom. These are the people whose journey's sometimes are destined to be short. He was sent to touch your soul but it really was his time to go back to heaven. Back to the Realms of Spirit from where he was sent from in the very beginning."

Darren seemed to settle a little in his thoughts for a while. I continued. "Keilyn doesn't want you to beat yourself up over those last moments. He wants you to understand. He was sent with his love to change your life and that his love and his spirit lives on. I have no doubt. He will continue to visit you and be 'around' you all and he will, without doubt be the first in line to greet you at the end of your journey. But your journey doesn't end yet, as you have been blessed with a lovely family that needs you very much."

I finally heard Keilyn beg his Daddy to 'stop'.

Darren sat with his head in his hands for a while as if he was trying to absorb everything that had been said. He stood up and shook my hand. He glanced at the spot where Keilyn had been standing. You could see he was struggling for words, when he said, "What can I say, other than... I could come here every day."

I shall never forget Keilyn. Not so much for the answers he gave with regards to the tragic circumstances in which he passed, but for the help and understanding he gave his Daddy.

That was not the last I saw of the beautiful boy Keilyn, as he came to visit once more, during another sitting some months later, this time he came to communicate to his beloved Auntie.

Keilyn introduced me to her too, so naturally and clear.

It is understandable that just like us, those in the

spirit would naturally know who their loved ones are.

A true Spirit's fundamental purpose would be to bring comfort to their loved ones here. It is the ability to give the answers in help in delivering an outcome to a case, but most of all, giving an understanding of the Spiritual Realms and its power of love. Keilyn was and is a very special little boy and a wonderful messenger. He is an absolute true Angel. May God Bless your pure Heart and soul.

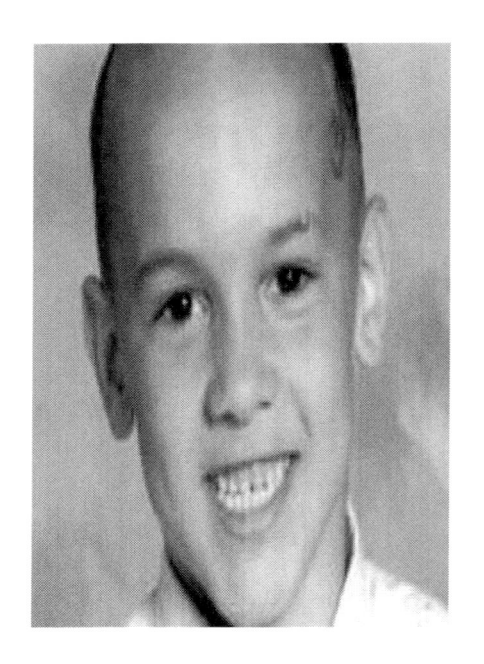

KEILYN KERR

MISSING

It wasn't unexpected to receive a phone call from the BBC local journalist Jules McCarthy, one October morning. Jules and I became acquainted after fate had brought her to one of my theatre shows where she received a detailed message from her beloved grandfather in spirit. Since then she has shown an avid interest in my work and my 'Gifts'.

She had phoned to ask, if I would spend the day with her on a visit to Shrewsbury, to see if I could give any insight to the whereabouts of a missing woman named Mandy Franks. She had been miss Nightclub in the Town Centre.

The case had begun to run cold and had left Detectives baffled. Jules suggested the following Thursday morning would be an ideal day to meet up, as it was the day before she was due to interview Police Detectives on an update on the case. I wasn't sure what her intentions were, I assumed she would relay any information received from my insights.

Again, something 'familiar' happened the night before we were due to travel to Shrewsbury. My sleep was interrupted by a 'vision'. Its timing told me it was connected to the disappearance of Mandy Franks.

I had a 'vision' of a Park, in the centre of which stood a large building. Most importantly, I could see the bow of a river flowing through the park. What intrigued me was the ornate design of benches which seemed to align the edge of the water. I just knew this park had something to do with Mandy's disappearance and was an important part of the equation.

We met up early on the Thursday morning. No sooner had we met, I informed Jules of the 'vision' that I'd had happened during my night's sleep.

"Wherever we go today, Jules, you must take me to a park, as I feel it has a connection to her disappearance... is there a big park in Shrewsbury?" I asked.

"Well actually there are a number of parks, unfortunately, it could be one of several." she told me.

"Oh well. We'll see when we get there then." I replied optimistically.

We drove the forty or so miles to Shrewsbury, and as we approached the Town Centre, making our way around the one-way system, my eyes caught a glimpse of a set of park gates, almost hidden by their surroundings.

I commanded Jules to stop the car. I was feeling very drawn to the area. Jules was eager to check it out. She told me that it was interesting that I should pinpoint that particular park. It was known as 'Quarry Park' and that particular park's location seemed to be situated behind the Nightclub, where Mandy was last seen leaving. The Nightclub was where Jules was initially planning to take me.

Jules decided she just couldn't wait; she had to take a look at what I was suggesting. She quickly parked the car, leaped out and ran ahead of me into the park. She beat me to it, as she was returning ,well before I could even reach the gates to see the full view. She approached me with a beaming smile on her face. It spoke volumes.

"You know what, Angela? It looks very much like what you described; It is this park which is renowned for the ornate design of its benches too, apparently. There's also a large boathouse building situated almost centrally, and you can see the bow of a river aligned with those ornate benches. Just as you said, it's uncanny. And the fact that it is so near to the Nightclub too. You're Amazing"…. She continued to build on a possible thesis.

"This may have been a route that Mandy possibly took if she had decided to walk home that night, as it leads in the direction to where she lived. Who knows? Let's go and see the Nightclub then." she insisted.

Jules suggested we come back to the park later, as she was eager to take me to the doors of the Nightclub, where Mandy was last seen on the CCTV camera, as she felt it may give me a 'beginning' to what actually happened that evening.

We got back in the car and continued to drive around the complex one way system, which seemed to take us in the opposite direction. Feeling a little bit disorientated, Jules parked up on a Car Park opposite the Nightclub. That is where I 'received' another 'vision', this time a reel of flashing visions, in which I 'saw' Mandy, leaving the nightclub. She appeared to be alone. She crossed over the road and came towards the car park were Jules and I were sat, parked up.

There was a man waiting in a car, a dark coloured saloon. Mandy approached the car and got in; she appeared to be arguing with the man. I sensed he was a man she knew. I could 'see' Mandy hastily getting out of the car, slamming the door and running down the side street adjacent, and not far from the nightclub's entrance. I described what I saw to Jules. Jules confirmed that the side street I pointed to, actually lead to the entrance of Quarry Park that we had visited moments earlier.

The man I saw in the car drove off. I asked Jules to start driving, so we could follow what my insights was showing me.

We had to drive in the opposite direction as we had to go with a one way flow of traffic. Inevitably it eventually led to the park gates, where the man in my 'vision' had parked up too, alongside some public toilets, and he had watched Mandy go into the park. This time, Jules and I were both prepared to enter the park together. Jules was making note of every word, recording it on a device. Everything that I was 'relaying', from my Guides and helpers.

I began to describe my 'visions'. I told Jules that it was raining heavily that fateful evening. It was lashing down, like torrential rain. I could 'see' the river as I entered the park; the river was overflowing, brimming over the sides with no clear edge to see. Mandy was followed into the park by this man who seemed to tower over her. The man grabbed her, he was arguing with her. There was a lot of pushing and shoving going on. Mandy was struck and fell into the river. My vision ended, I felt I had an answer. I then found myself standing next to the edge of the river and becoming aware of my own presence within the park, that sunny autumn morning. I glanced at my feet. The river was still this time, a total contrast to what it was that night. I had the dreadful feeling of a realisation.

"Mandy's body went into the river here," I pointed….. "I'm sorry to say… the body went into the water, Jules." I insisted.

Jules looked deep in thought.

"She's in the water, Jules." I repeated myself again and again. I then paused, waiting for a response.

"No, Angela…" came the reply.

Jules frowned and looked puzzled. She informed me that this stretch of river, had already been searched by

Police Frogmen, and nothing was found. Jules seemed to be dismissing my thoughts. This threw me little. But persistent as usual, I found I was repeating myself again. The thoughts was being replayed in my mind over and over. I had not to give up on this trail of thought.

After all, I had full trust in my Guides, even though there were doubts, although they weren't mine.

It was then I had another 'vision' together with some conclusive thoughts given to me again by Spirit.

"Jules.. I said... "Mandy's body is definitely in this water and it went in here at this point in the park. It was carried by the strong current, but wherever this river loops around a very small town, that is where her body lies. I sense she's still in the water. And this is where she will be found, Bless her."

I then had a 'vision' of the small town in question as it appeared clear in my mind's eye. I continued as Jules made notes and listened attentively to me

" There is a part of the river that appears to be edged by a tall wall, situated close by is a church with a blue domed roof on top of its tower."

Jules interrupted me by saying she thought she knew where this small town was. My description sounded familiar "It sounds like Bridgnorth to me. But that's about twenty miles away!" she remarked sounding doubtful again.

Then I said something which surprised us both. A 'prophetic' thought came in out of the blue, "You know what, Jules, that IS where Mandy will be found, but it won't be till next week, whilst I'm on holiday."

Why on earth did I make that statement, I thought. God only knows. Jules noted it all the same. She knew I had planned to go away on holiday the following week to Ireland.

After that statement I had to remind myself of the 'blind faith' I must carry at all times. Sometimes it's hard, as much as I know.

Although I continued to repeat the description of the place I 'saw' in my vision, I still needed that psychical reassurance of what I'd received. I suggested that on our return that day, I would try and draw a sketch of what I saw, which Jules had likened to Bridgnorth. I need not have doubted or asked for the paper, as when we returned back home, before I got chance to draw a sketch, Jules' daughter recognised and gave further confirmation too. We also found matching photographic evidence from images on the Internet, which not only confirmed that it was definitely Bridgnorth but we also found photographs of the renowned ornate benches belonging to Quarry Park in Shrewsbury too.

This gave me a wonderful sense of hope. There were more results to come, as in similar cases like these, and still they never fail to cease to amaze, even me.

In the days that followed I got to hear that Jules had

mentioned my findings to the Police Detectives involved in the case, the following day. Their response was not unexpected, as not every Police Detective decides to 'think outside the box.' In this case they seemed to listen to what Jules had to say about my findings, as they said it was a 'very feasible' explanation to what may have happened to Mandy that night.

I found it to be a reasonable response as many officers are non-believers in the Spiritual Realms existence, as fundamentally their work conditions them to think with hard facts and logic. But for Officers who do take a chance, they are surprised and educated. It basically boils down to the individual officer's belief system whether to 'accept' or 'explore' this type of information

I would have loved to of been 'a fly on the wall' watching their reaction though, the following week. In fact it was six days later. Whilst I was still on holiday, I had a text from my Journalistic colleague and friend Jules McCarthy, stating that the body of Mandy Franks was found in the river of the small town of Bridgnorth, exactly where and when I had stated it would be found. I just hoped that it opened up those minds of those sceptical officers when they read the newspaper headline: 'MEDIUM GIVES LOCATION TO MISSING WOMAN'S BODY'.

For me it was a continued lesson to remind myself never to doubt my 'visions'. There have been remarkable ones over the years but all have come with great purpose, unfolding knowledge and giving valuable information and confirmation. But most of all, in this case a good result, helping to bring some closure to a broken-hearted family and Mandy to a final resting place. God rest her soul.

This case proves yet again that not only answers can be obtained but very positive results too with the right help, acceptance and most of all Belief.

Which leads me to...

Ornate Benches, Quarry Park

River and Church, Bridgnorth

MADDIE

It was one day whilst I was going about my daily chores. I began to receive vivid 'visions' and thoughts, that I couldn't make sense of, or connect with anything that had recently been drawn to my attention. Still, I knew they had come for a purpose and reason.

    I was 'seeing' a picture of white painted apartments with vertical shutters on the windows. Wherever it was, was in sunnier climes. I felt a great sense of danger when I 'saw' a man with dark, almost shoulder length hair. He was a disheveled looking man with a very prominent v-shaped hairline. I saw him leaving , carrying a little girl. I knew these visions were in a far off place somewhere abroad.

    Whilst images continued to flash repeatedly in my mind, I 'sensed' he took the little girl to a place nearby, where there was a large concrete building that looked like unfinished blocks of apartments or a car park. I sensed he then, he drove her to a place in a hillside outside a small isolated village.

I was puzzled by these 'visions'. What did they mean? I wondered if perhaps what I was being 'shown' was something about to unfold on the American 'Afterlife' radio show, which I was still recording each weekend.

It wasn't until the following day when I realised what it all meant.

Again it was Jules McCarthy who phoned me to arrange an interview on BBC radio but on a different matter.

It was almost at the end of our conversation that she seemed prompted by a final thought and question:

"Did you hear the news yesterday...about the little girl in Portugal who has gone missing?"

"No, BUT!" I almost shouted, remembering the 'visions' I had experienced the day before.

I explained that yesterday was one of those rare days I had allocated to myself. I had planned to rest, having the day off in the peace and quiet of my home, being oblivious to the world outside.

"Oh Jules, I must tell you something," I said, "I received a spate of 'visions'. It is all to do with the little girl you're mentioning. I'm convinced."

I told her about my 'visions' and I started to have more thoughts on the matter. I knew that as Jules was Journalist first and foremost, I had no doubt she was making notes on what I was saying. I continued to tell her of my feelings and thoughts as to what was going to happen in this case.

I felt that there was a man with a German girlfriend, who lived close by to the apartments, who would get involved somehow in the process of enquiries. Also , that there would be a 'finger of suspicion' pointed at the parents as their conduct had some proportion to the blame.

As the weeks went by the information I 'received' unfolded. A good Medium can only give what they receive. And it is within a great sense of duty that my experiences needed to be noted too, I felt.

I didn't realise then that my connection with this case on day two, would continue, with intervening messages and 'visions' over a period of two years at very poignant times, giving more information each time, reinforcing a validity to my 'connections'.

I hoped that what I had received would be noted with God's help by giving the McCann family answers that they so needed, it is only a matter of time. I do believe in the power of prayer. And God knows how I've prayed for them, in this case.

The unfortunate thing about this case is that it drew nearly every Psychic and Medium in the world to give an answer. I didn't set out to give any answers; I had no choice in the matter. I understand there have been many pieces of information that have been 'received' by Psychics, Mediums and alike, from all around the world. I understand those that wrote in, about their own insights, have been filed but I can imagine many people, who are clearly not psychic, wrote in too, creating confusion and a smoke screen to the genuine Psychics and Mediums in the world. This issue made me feel somewhat reluctant and helpless, but it seemed that events happened to help me surge my insights into the media in hope that it would filter through to the appropriate people. Writing about this now is still part of that process.

My attention was drawn to this case yet again approximately six months later, when my first book was released. An interview with the Birmingham *Sunday Mercury* had been arranged in hope of grasping a good review. One of the main talking points of my book seemed to be the chronicled accounts of my Psychic Detective work, which had gained recognition from Detective Chief Inspector Ian Bamber of West Midlands Police, who appeared on television to talk about my abilities and 'visions', and my involvement in a local murder case in which he was the Chief Officer in charge at the time. He later gave permission to endorse my book with a wonderful quote taken from the TV series in which we had both appeared in.

But it was a few nights before the scheduled interview with the Sunday Mercury, that I was woken from my sleep by the sounds of a little girl crying. I recognised her as Madeleine McCann. I sat up as the 'vision' seemed to waken me. I appeared to be looking down at a map. I could see a forked road, almost like a right angled triangle with Monchchique' written in the middle, a name which I thought sounded very French. Maybe she was in France, I thought., but then another vision flashed up. This time it was a landscape picture with boulders to the left-hand corner, barren land in the foreground, a line of tall trees all set within a hillside - it was rather picturesque. I felt that Maddie was near a small remote village within a hillside. Her pleas were echoing in my mind as I found myself fully awake finding tears rolling down my cheeks. I felt so distraught and frustrated. I wanted to help but I didn't know how to do that. I knew these 'visions' where connected to Maddie, but didn't know what to do about them.

The sense of urgency and desperation' decided for me. I did something completely out of my nature. I immediately went downstairs to my computer and logged on to the Gerry McCann website (Maddie's father). I wrote Gerry a message telling him, that I was a genuine Medium who has had worked with Police and that I had recent 'visions' of Maddie. I left him my contact number. I just couldn't carry the burden of it any longer, as I just had to take action, thinking it was the right thing to do.

Sadly, there was no acknowledgement from him. I did what I thought was right at that time but there again I must have been one of many tens of thousands who have logged a message on that site, and thousands of a Psychic nature.

A few days later the journalist from the *Sunday Mercury* arrived at my home to interview me about my book. The interview went very well, I felt. The journalist had obviously had done his homework about my past work but just as the interview was coming to a close; he asked me a more topical question.

"Have you ever 'received' anything about Madeleine McCann?" he said very inquisitively.

His question had come as a surprise but it had perfect timing attached to it. I began to explain about my 'connections' and told him of my recent 'visions' from a few days before.

"That's interesting…"

He continued to make notes; He asked nothing else, shook my hand to thank me and then left.

On the following Sunday morning, I went to buy a copy of the newspaper, hoping for a good book review. I was shocked when I saw a lead from the front page making headlines: what seemed to be a purported Headline which ..read.. 'MADDIE SPOKE TO ME' - by Police Psychic.

I was by baffled, how could the newspaper could conjure up such a headline. I stood there reading the article before I'd even paid for the paper, such was my suspense. From what I read, it seemed my book was less important and my 'visions' about Maddie were paramount. According to the press, the 'visions' I had substantiated, amounted to some important facts, unbeknown to me.

It confirmed that Monchique is a small village almost

untouched by tourism and is set in a hillside, which is situated 30 minutes' drive away from Praid Du Luz where Maddie went missing. The most interesting part is that the press said that there had been reports 'leaked' to them, by a German pedophile, that was presently serving sentence in a Dutch prison. This man had confessed that a pedophile ring had been operating in that same village; it was something that the press stated and added that I could not have been aware of, as it had not been made public. I then felt justified in what I had received, but not necessarily justified how it was exposed in the media. I was upset, as the article made reference to Maddie's 'Body' too. I can understand a lay person's confusion, as my 'visions' are not always of people who have 'crossed over'. The reporter, I felt, had made an assumption as I also receive 'visions' of people in the 'living' sense too.

Further confirmation on the case came months later, when a revised edition of my book was released by a new publisher, Hayhouse.

I was on a visit to London for an interview with the *Daily Mail* after which I planned to visit family who lived on the other side of the City. When I arrived I had an unexpected call from my publisher, to see if I would do an unscheduled interview with Steve Kitchen on BBC Radio Gloucester the following morning, to which I agreed.

The timing was very poignant. I didn't know that the headline news across all the Media that morning would become a topic in my interview. It was the day that

Portuguese Police, after approximately 18 months had passed, they released a photo-fit description of a possible suspect for the very first time. He was a man who had been seen hanging around the apartments in Praid du Luz at time of Maddie's disappearance.

Why they chose to release it nearly eighteen months after the disappearance, I will never understand. I shuddered when I saw the photo-fit of this man; it was splashed all over the national newspapers.

It was the disheveled looking man with a prominent v-shaped hairline which fitted my description from one of my earliest 'visions' on day two of the investigation.

During the interview that morning, I was asked about Madeleine McCann, which I half expected. Steve asked if I had seen the photo-fit picture that morning and my opinion of it. I informed him that I had given a similar description to a BBC news journalist, on day two of the enquiry.

My interview certainly gave 'food for thought' about the way the case was handled and made 'Pick of the day' news for the *Radio Gloucester* website.

More surprises were planned ahead by my helpers and Guides in the spirit world. More coincidences, synchronicities and actual validations continued to happen, bringing more attention to the 'visions' that I had with regards to this case, confirming, and reaffirming my Faith each time.

Some months later, I was in a conversation with a high-ranking detective named Geoff (who will remain anonymous by his request).

I had not seen him for a period of time. He was another officer who was very much aware of my abilities and my work. My 'Gifts' have been used and noted by numerous Detectives and Officers to date, but most of my work involving such cases remains confidential.

We were actually talking of another case, when Geoff realised and remarked that it had been at least two years since we last met.

He then asked the most expected question, when he realised that one of the 'biggest' cases ever reported had happened since our last meeting.

"Did you ever get anything about Maddie?" he asked.

"Well, it's interesting you should say that," I replied.

I then went into great detail, explaining all my 'visions' and thoughts that I had received from the start. Geoff's response was to show interest in my latest vision of the map and the picture of the hillside.

"Have you *Google Earthed* it?" he asked.

"What do you mean?" I said. I had forgotten about the computer program *Google Earth,* as I had heard about it but never used it. So Geoff kindly directed me step-by-step through the download procedure. (I am not so much technical as I am spiritual please note, I thought.)

As I trawled the arrows across the map of Europe, I came across Portugal and searched for Praid du Luz and around its perimeter. I spotted the area of the Monchique Mountains. I then saw a small dot representing the village of Monchique. I felt nervous as I 'zoomed' in on the dot. The map unfolded in front of my eyes, there was the right angled triangular forked shaped road with Monchique written in the middle, just as I had seen in my 'vision'.

I then trawled the arrows across into the hillside, where I saw a little 'square' this time, not a dot, but an indicator all the same.

It was obviously indicating something, so I opened that up too. I was expecting to see a residential area but I found that the little 'square' on the map represented a tourist picture. I was shocked to find that it was exactly the picture which had been 'shown' to me in my other 'vision' that night. It was of the boulders and the Barron land, that was short of 'amazing' too.

As for Geoff, when I told him, he was not so surprised as he trusted my 'works'.

"You can't just let this go. You need to get over there. Shame there are so many 'Psychics' spoiling it, for genuine people like you."

I knew exactly what he meant.

"Can you imagine if I did go there and the things unfolded?" I said as I imagined myself in Portugal. "I wouldn't be informing Portuguese police though. I would have to wait to come home and tell the police here. I wish I could, Geoff. All I know is these 'visions' weren't given to me for no reason at all..."

I made Geoff a half promise to commit myself to this cause, to put any information I received 'out there' in the best way that I could. I knew I would, with a little help from my heavenly 'friends' .

This episode dismissed my niggling doubts, and yet again it made me feel very humble. My 'visions' had been confirmed once again. I have no doubt that like all my visions, they had real and true purpose.

It was a shortly after that I was invited on the Chris Baxter show on BBC Radio Leicester at 9am, which was considered radio 'prime time' as it would reach people including those on a 'school run'. It was a scheduled interview about my Psychic Detective work. The aim of the interview was in hope of some way, subtly, drawing my name to the attention of the McCann family as they had now returned back to their home town of Leicester.

Sadly the case continued unsolved amidst a barrage of conflicting information by good meaning people worldwide but my attention was drawn to it yet again. Kate and Gerry McCann were making headlines yet again but this time it was about their own case against the Portuguese Police

Officer in Charge of the enquiry with reference to his inappropriate 'handling' of the case. They questioned the procedures and decisions he had made during the early stages of the investigation.

This was the subject of the front page headline that came to my attention. It was a copy of the Sun newspaper, a paper I would not normally choose to read. I was sitting at a table in a small café waiting to be served. What caught my eye even more, was the sub heading: 'KATE MCCANN HAD A DREAM'. I was then tempted to look.

It stated that days after Maddie's disappearance Kate confessed that she had a dream that her daughter was in a hillside.

A tear cam e to my eyes. I felt that this was a very poignant 'sign', a personal message for me, reiterating what I had received. I recognised that in the first few days of the enquiry there had been a dual 'message' from spirit, a parallel message, sent to both Kate McCann and I

I feel this chapter had to be written. What I have written about this case is out of pure love and respect for Kate and Gerry McCann and their family, nothing else. I pray to God to bless them with answers to their prayers, for I have no doubt that the hillside of the Monchique Mountains holds answers too.

MONCHIQUE

BARREN LAND

MICHAEL

Michael Bentine's wonderful work as a medium seemed to go unnoticed. He was mostly renowned for the zany side of his comic character, which he displayed for many years on BBC Radio comedy classic *The Goon Show*.

But it was the knowledge of his so-called 'sensitive' side I was to find out about, a number of years after his death amidst some very traumatic circumstances that was bought to my notice..

At the end of one of my Theatre Shows, during a book signing, I was approached discreetly, by middle-aged lady, who told me her name was Deirdre.

I remembered I had called her name, during the show apparently, and had given her a message from her late father. She asked if I could spare some time to help her, but She stated she didn't need a sitting as such. She asked if it was possible for me to find a spare few hours in my busy schedule but at short notice, preferably whilst I was in the area, as she wished to take me to a location that was near. She said she needed some help and confirmation on something. I understood her intentions clearly and the privacy attached to her request, but I sensed her desperation and turmoil too.

With this in mind, I discreetly gave her my details of

where to contact me. Luckily, it just so happened that the evening was the last in the tour and I could be available before my return home the following day. I felt obliged to help because of its timing, and the fact that spirit had already spoken to her in a message. I .naturally agreed to meet her as it seemed to have been instrumented by my Guides that I do so.

She came to collect me from the Hotel where I was staying the following morning. There was a bitter chill in the wind that day. Deirdre arrived holding what appeared to be frayed files of paper. She held them close to her chest. I looked down at them as if waiting for an explanation. She said that she dare not leave them in the car as they hold crucial information.

She carefully locked them back into the boot of her car as we left. Deirdre then drove miles into the countryside, where we came to an old derelict gatehouse building that stood at the opening of the road, which led into a woodland area. Deirdre told me it was once privately owned but it has recently become a very popular place to walk, especially for residents of a new housing estate, that had recently been built close by.

We parked up the car. Deirdre grabbed the frayed paper files out the boot and walked with them, gripping them, holding them close. It was obvious she did not want them out of her sight for long. Our conversation was brief and polite. We both knew what my purpose was for being there. As we trudged through the undergrowth there were many dips to the landscape, which unveiled roots of trees and craggy surroundings. I felt I was being led, though not by Deirdre.

The Woods were quite dense, we were almost central, surrounded by trees in every direction. I glanced down at a large area of ground, which seemed to dipped many feet lower much to where we found ourselves standing.

I had a vision, whilst looking at the lower ground. It seemed to be very, very bizarre; I had never 'witnessed' anything like this before. In the vision there were several people standing around, forming a circle.

The people were wearing masks. There were seven of them, two were females. They seem to be making very strange gestures, almost like dancing. In the middle of their circle stood two small children, a boy and a girl, who were clinging to each other with fear, crying, clearly petrified.

I stood in silence, I was clearly stunned. Deirdre was watching my every move and reaction. She saw the look of shock on my face as I explained, "Look, I can only tell you what I see and what I see doesn't make sense." I stuttered.

I was strangely unnerved. Deirdre could understand my hesitation. My confidence was being knocked purely because of the 'sight' it was so horrible and bizarre.

"Please just tell me as it is." she begged.

"I see a number of people encircling two small children.

A boy and a girl of about the age of five or six years old. The people surrounding them are wearing masks. There are five men and two women." I said. I felt it had happened a couple of decades ago, or so.

Deirdre's face seemed grief stricken. Her eyes filled with tears. "Those were my children." she sobbed.

She explained that one day her little boy had made a disclosure about his and his sister's 'plight' whilst drawing.

Deirdre told me, "They had both drawn separately, very innocently, a number of graphic pictures, of the events. In hindsight, I knew one of the predators was my husband, their father at the time. I then pieced together a number of past events and strange behaviors involving him, that I questioned, and we had argued over, at the time. But he seemed to convince me it was my imagination and at times accused me of being somewhat deranged. One such thing that stuck in my mind was that my dresses would go missing from my wardrobe and mysteriously reappear days later. It was through further disclosure I realised my 'missing' dresses were part of a ploy to prevent the children from disclosing. Making them think that they had no one to turn to as it seemed to them, that one of the women abusing them, was their mother too, as one of the perpetrators had worn my stolen dresses during their evil acts." Deirdre's tears flowed down her cheeks, which she seemed to ignore as if all had been in vain.

My heart sank and my stomach churned. The anger of

the injustice struck a familiar chord deep to the core of my being. I felt like a helpless child wanting to fight her corner.

Even in all my years of working in Child Protection, I had only come across one such case that had hinted at, what is labeled as 'Satanic Worship' abuse. It was never proven, but suspicions were high amongst the Officials at all levels at t my workplace, although without adding my 'unconventional' insights. It all appeared so obvious but all so very hard to prove legally. I had no doubt Deirdre's case was true, as further confirmation began to build up.

Deirdre went on to explain that the case had actually gone to court. Such a case during that time was exceptionally rare, almost unheard of. The social and legal system back then, wasn't even beginning to recognise Child Sexual abuse let alone that of 'Satanic' worship. Only cases of physical abuse and neglect were often recorded and dealt with then.

Deirdre continued, "Back in those days there was no Child Psychologist involved, as there would be now. So as you might guess, the case got thrown out of Court and I was labeled by the Judge as a 'neurotic woman'. The judge seemed appalled that I would bring such a case to court. Let alone have the audacity to accuse such ' Pillars of society' of such a thing. I still have all the files and those graphic pictures too. You only have to look at them to know the truth. I will show you them later."

I began to receive thoughts and more visions. I gave her

two names, and occupations of two of the perpetrators, which she confirmed, which related to two of the accused. I then had a 'vision' of a church on a hill which I said was also significant to those 'graphic' events which had been drawn up.

"You're exactly right," she said. "I will take you there next."

We drove to the church which appeared to be quite isolated and aged. It was surrounded by a graveyard with dilapidated headstones. The church itself was locked, just as we expected. It also appeared to have been a target for vandals. We walked round the body of the Church, almost full circle. I noticed I'd stopped and became aware I was outside the doors which lead to the most sacred part of the church, the Altar. It was then I had a very graphic vision. It became obvious to me that some of the children's abuse took place inside the church. All of which was confirmed by Deirdre.

I felt physically sick as more details flowed to my consciousness. But at the same time, I was more conscious of Deirdre's feelings, which were paramount. We found a bench amongst the headstones and sat down. It was there that Deirdre made a grand gesture of handing me her paper files. They were the legal files and court details of the case with the additional, forgotten but crucial, unmistakable evidence, as pinned to the back of the file were those graphic, heart-breaking pictures drawn through the 'lost innocence' of her two small children. We sat isolated, in an empty churchyard above a small town. We were totally alone in our thoughts, knowing that there were few people who knew the real truth about what happened all those years ago. I sat reading the file for quite a while and thought that one day, the truth will unfold but it would take time.

I became aware of a communication from a gentleman in the spirit world. He seemed to echo the same sentiments that I had just said.

"Who is the man with wavy dark hair and a beaming smile?" I asked. "He appears to be always laughing. You know Deidre, he reminds me of someone. He looks like Michael Bentine, you know him out of The *Goons*." Deidre smiled for the first time. "This man I sense has a connection with you, but I don't feel he's family. He's trying to tell you the truth will unfold."

Deirdre grabbed my hand. "I know exactly who you mean; there is no other person it could be. It was another Medium who I'd asked for help with this case. It was actually Michael Bentine of *The Goons* fame. I wrote to him and he kindly agreed to help me too. He also gave me wonderful evidence and came to the same conclusions as you."

That did surprise me. To say that Michael Bentine's gentle spirit echoed a 'supporting' message which was just another touching moment, to a very humbling day.

DEATH

The hardest lesson we have to learn in life's process is death, the death of a loved one. The words death and dead sound so final. I prefer to choose the words 'crossed over'.

'Crossed over' or 'passed over' is a term people often used, quite often without knowing the true and deeper meaning. Having knowledge of the Spiritual Realms can give us the greatest comfort during these times. It is a fact that during these times some people will only really start to think and question the concept of God and the Afterlife for the very first time.

'Loosing' a loved one is inevitable. We all have to go through grief eventually, but some earlier than others and some more often.

Death is the only thing that unites us all, although the pain of grief tends to isolate us. It can make us feel separate not only from our loved ones but sometimes from those around us. We tend to withdraw into ourselves, becoming needy and ultra-sensitive. We withdraw into the core of our being, our soul. We drift in and out of this state for an unspecified period of time, with an added roller-coaster of emotions that becomes a permanent part of our lives. Sometimes it's like being hit by an unexpected tidal wave with a fear of the next one. With a roller-coaster of grief's emotions, the pain it creates is something we consider unbearable, we cannot escape it and find it very hard to express. Death, we are never truly prepared for it.

Death of a loved one, always appears untimely, even in the expected latter years of our lives. No matter how much we educate ourselves about life, death is still treated in many aspects, as a taboo subject. It can be our biggest fear.

Death is one of most difficult things to accept in life, if not the hardest. It is in our state of grief we feel the greatest pain but at the same time, it is within that emotion we feel the greatest love, caused by the 'want of who we yearn for. It is within that state that God and our loved ones draw close to us.

Eventually, in our own time, we learn to pocket those emotions but it is only time that sometimes seems to 'heal' us from our loss. Time will eventually put a wedge between the initial traumas of our loved ones passing and ease us into thinking more of the life we shared with them. The only true comfort and solace some people get within grief, as a newly found belief in God is the concept of an Afterlife or both.

Often, for those people who lack beliefs or a lack of an understanding, their loss may seem greater. Loss itself will often trigger them to questioning the process of death, the 'meaning of life' and they often become a seeker; this inevitably draws them closer to the infinite power of God.

It is when we are struggling with those conditions of grief that we withdraw inwardly into the core of our souls, seeking and searching for reason. It is then, when unbeknownst to some, we in our inwardly state are actually making a subconscious connection to the Highest Realm. During that time, almost oblivious to us, we are given an answer through an 'encounter' a spiritual experience of some sort, which we may not fully notice or understand but it will make us question, never the less.

It is those inward feelings of our grief that sensitizes us to receiving spirit communication from the higher realms, from our loved ones in particular. I have no doubt that our loved ones would want to comfort us during this time and beyond. The feeling of their presence would tell us that all is well with them and that they have continued to live on in some way. Quite often whilst witnessing an encounter it is often accompanied by an overwhelming feeling instilled within in us ,which is one of love and peace.

I recall time and time again, people who have said they had sailed through life as non-believers until someone close to them' crossed over'. During their feelings of 'isolation' they had some sort of experience of spiritual kind. An experience that they could not explain but it changed their concept of life and death completely

People from all walks of life will talk about their spiritual experiences, some openly as if they had discovered gold for the time. Others will tell you about it in the strictest of confidence, as if they fear they may be ridiculed in some way or belittled for the lack of understanding.

Some people's experiences have been totally, life changing. I would say that each and every one of us will encounter an experience of a spiritual kind during the process of their lives, and that encounter will trigger an awakening. Even if it is only at the time when they are taking their very own 'last breath' in life, it may be then that they will realize they are entering another 'Realm'.

All Spiritual Realms are of the same source and cannot be separated. As God is the creator of all things...

I personally have witnessed and heard of so many life changing experiences due to intervention of spirit and spirit communication, that there is no doubt in my mind that we can gain guidance, advice and help in many ways through our connection with Spirit of the highest - which is God.

GIFTS OF THE SOUL

I was once asked what one aspect of my Gift of communication, I find the most valuable, whether it was 'seeing', 'hearing', 'sensing' spirit, or my Prophecy and 'visions'.

In answer I would say my 'visions' would just 'pip the others at the post'. These visions seem most valuable when used at the scene of crimes but all aspects have relevant use and guises for purpose and reason but all are one of the same, a communication.

In the past I have been taken by Police Detectives to specific locations and given no information to why. I am then asked what I 'sense' and 'feel' in that particular area. This is when almost on cue; I begin to receive my 'visions'. My 'visions' are not necessarily of people of the spirit world. They are often of living people too. I sometimes get to 'see' the culprits in action. I watch snippets, seconds of re-enactments which seemed set on a 'silk-screen' within my mind's eye, which is reflected on top of what is psychically there. It's like watching a video recording of findings and maybe the culprits, doing their evil deeds. The reason I think I get a few seconds at a time, is that it is just enough time to comprehend and relay the information without leaving any heavy psychological and emotional effects within my persona. It is spirits way of protecting me also keeping me safe. It is short and distant, not allowing any confusion with any possible memory or reality that I have lived or known of.

Quite often my 'visions' would be coupled with a communication from the murder victim's spirit. They sometimes return to the scene to help give further assistance.

I can only describe my 'visions' as divine intervention. I am left feeling humbled. My understanding is that it comes from the highest vibration of the heavenly Realms, God's Realm. That of 'light' and good.

I have also grasped over the years, a good understanding of the 'other' labels that people have placed on me. But there is still a lot of confusion about defining the words Psychic, Medium and Visionary and the understanding of the true meaning.

I believe we are all capable of being what we call 'Psychic'. Being psychic is a natural process which stems from our spirit body. If we examine the meaning of Psychic, from which we get the word Psyche, we discover is derives from the Greek word for soul, another name for spirit. So within us all is the soul, the spirit body, which is the core of our being. The soul enters into the psychical body at conception, it is the God given life form. It is this same spirit body that transcends back to the realms of spirit in the process of so called death.

We can all get attuned to our souls, our psyche, our inner-self. Call it what you may.

We recognise and listen to those thoughts and feelings coming from our 'psyche', which naturally penetrates through our psychical body and mind, recognising the reactions it causes. It becomes known as our 'sixth sense', our intuition. After all it is a part of us, as natural as any other.

People who recognize and understand this to a higher degree, will be able to work with those reactions and feelings, these people are called Psychics. It may have taken years to discover or even a lifetime to discover that knowledge that sense from within.

Psychics that are in the process of self-discovery often need tools to draw on or help to project and reflect those feelings and thoughts, almost like a crutch. But there again those feelings and thoughts are only coming from within their own spirit body and within a natural process, during which they may receive some intervals of 'Mediumistic' experiences.

Mediumship is a different aspect, but is like an

extension, a progression, a development from the same foundation and source. I see it as a 'gift' of the soul.

There are many gifts we receive at birth and during our life span. We all have gifts within us. It is whether in this life, we discover those gifts and have the chance to nurture and express them.

When your soul is able to receive messages from other souls from other Realms, it is then that you are actually working on a higher 'level'. Many Psychics receive episodes of these types of messages. I feel it is at this stage in their development when some people get confused and call themselves a Medium and understandably so. But it is only true Mediumship when ALL your messages and ALL the information you receive come from the souls in the highest realms of spirit and not from within your own Psyche – (your soul). You will naturally learn to know the difference and will not need to use any 'tools' as such at that higher level. When you are able to recognise the difference in the levels and that it can be expressed as a continuous process, then that is the clear meaning of someone who is a true Medium.

Mediumship cannot be given to someone else as such, you can be taught awareness on how to develop and recognise your own stage of spiritual awareness in the process of discovering and nurturing your own 'connections'.

This is why so-called lay people, people who seek

assistance, those who are searching for answers, love and comfort from their loved ones, get confused and disheartened because of the people they go to, are often confused themselves, not the process and progress of the Psyche and its development and the manifestation of true Gifts. Put simply, not all Psychics are Mediums but 'true' Mediums would fundamentally be naturally Psychic.

The development from Psychic to medium entails many different factors. These factors reflect in the way we progress in our lives and explore the natural process of our journey. Some people are born, an open 'channel', born with a 'gift' and others enhance their 'channel' through their life's experiences and self-development. I would call myself a natural born medium; I with hindsight, believe I was born an 'open' as such', a 'receiver' a messenger. Someone who was born with the wisdom of the Afterlife. This will be reflected, as a result of a recollection of previous lives and a spiritual evolution.

My mediumship developed naturally, through life's twist and turns, traumas and tragedies. It is in those traumatic and tragic times that you become so connected to the 'unseen'. It is when nothing in this physical world can help you. You will often will withdraw into a subconscious state of mind. It is then in those moments you are connecting to the higher realms and are given the 'understanding' and the knowledge of the spirit world, as we turn to God and the spiritual Realms and loved ones for help, almost naturally.

It was during those times in my life I have been given some of the greatest evidence and knowledge. So you see, the development of this gift of 'knowledge' and 'understanding' has not come easy. You could say, unfortunately, as those moments have been many. But fortunately for me, I hold no regrets or bitterness; for I grasped the reason why and understand that I have been blessed to be shown the wonders of' Universal energy' known as God.

Then there is the gift of healing. Healing is a word that encompasses all aspects of being, being able to receive the nurture of God's healing power. Healing is not necessarily 'hands on'.

We can heal people with our actions, our thoughts and our prayers and our deeds.

How often have we prayed for someone? Those thoughts are part of the spiritual healing process that can instrument a change. A thought has 'energy' and a power. The power of prayer is a wonderful thing. I have been witness to its results as it can heal, not only to help heal sick people but situations too.

It is the power of prayer too, that is used to release those lost and troubled souls, 'energies' that sometimes remain, get disturbed and discovered and are found amongst everyday life. Spiritual being, souls, 'energies,' some of have been left behind, or have left a remain, by leaving part of their 'energy' on the earthly plane. It is like leaving a stain on the energy field. Some 'energies may have been disturbed or called upon. There is sometimes an element of fear attached to such discoveries by people but it is the fear of the unknown that gives it an edge. Only the power of prayer that will disperse the ' energies, the souls,' and enables them to be released, to make transition to the appropriate Spirit Realm..

The process used in the release of such 'energies.' This is what I call a 'Soul Rescue' as I have helped or enabled souls to be released from earthly bounds to a Realm in which they are destined to return to, so that they can rest in peace and the people here can disperse their fear and gain peace of mind. Such 'soul rescues' have been an inevitable part of my work as a Medium. (The number of 'Soul Rescues' I have been involved with to date, have given me enough 'platform' to write a specialised book, on such a 'healing' subject).

There is many aspects to healing. Healing is in many forms. How often have we psychically touched someone when they have been hurt? This natural reaction of 'touch' is one of healing too.

Mediumship is a form of healing, as we give people comforting words, words of peace that brings solace. We are a spiritual channel, words are often being inspired. When we listen in counsel, we help to lift and heal people's pains, as counselling is a gift too.

I became aware of the 'healing power' after each of my

sittings many years ago. When a common response from people would be that they felt so much better, so much at peace afterwards. I pray each time I 'counsel' with my Mediumship, that people leave me feeling comforted and uplifted but most of all that they leave with peace of mind and spirit.

I have never professed to be a healer, a 'hands on' healer as such. Again this type of healing I have been a witness to and have received healing myself, many times. It makes sense that if you are 'channel', you are 'simply' able to 'receive'. You would be able to receive and channel God's ultimate power of healing .

It was only by request, that I first realized the connection within my Mediumship gift, many years ago. Healing in the true sense of the word is its accomplice. As God's healing power will pass through the same channel. If it is part of our journey to receive God's healing power, so be it.

I first recognised the ultimate healing connection, when I was asked by a woman, if I would lay my hands on her back. The request came after giving service in Church; she explained she had a painful back condition, that she had suffered with for some weeks.

I was surprised by the request, as it was so unexpected. I had never been asked before, but I obliged all the same.

Feeling a little inadequate from being inexperienced from this sort of request, I told her I didn't profess to be a 'hands on' healer but a channel all the same, so I was willing to try. Very simply, I placed my hands on her head and said a prayer in God's name and in Jesus's mane, I asked for healing to be given. It felt a natural thing to do, after asking her name.

I was shocked to get a phone call the next day from the same woman, stating that her back pain had gone. I cannot say that I didn't question it. But all the same I instantly reminded her that she must realize, it wasn't actually me, that gave her healing but the power of God.

I asked myself why I should question the power of healing and why didn't I question my Mediumship equally and my other Gifts too? Maybe it was the fact that those other gifts had been with me for such a long time, that it seemed such a natural part of my persona, as I have lived with it for all of my days.

It seemed it was time I had to recognise the 'reception' of the ultimate healing power within us all, so the spirit world seemed to be telling me.

The second incident that drew my attention was no doubt 'instrumented' too. I had gone to my local Town Hall after insightful circumstances drew me to an event. It was an evening of Clairvoyance with Medium Stephen O'Brien. I had a premonition that I would receive a message from him. And to no surprise, he gave me a message from my Great Uncle George, which held important reference, he also thanked me for the work I did for spirit. This made the audience aware of who I was.

It was in the interval, I was approached by a lady. She asked me if I was a Healer as well as a Medium, and did I live locally.

Again finding myself in a similar situation, I found myself explaining once again, that I did not profess to be a healer as such, yet again I found myself obliging as I knew this is what 'spirit' expected of me.

This time I arranged to travel to her home. Her name was Christine; she said she had suffered with a chronic chest condition, which had affected her breathing and as a consequence her mobility too. She had suffered from Emphysema for a number of years, which is an incurable illness.

Again I was feeling a little bit apprehensive; even more so than the last time to tell the truth. When I arrived at her home, I spent time talking to her, as she lay down on her bed. I laid my hands on her and said my prayers. I reminded her, if it was God's will for her to receive a healing, so be it. It seemed like I was hedging my bets. I always seem to preach about having 'blind' faith. Maybe mine was faltering at the time and I needed that reminder. I also gave her a loving message from her mother in spirit.

Christine remarked about the feeling of heat, she felt coming from my hands. I seemed surprised myself, I don't know why. I left, thinking I had done my duty to Spirit by giving her an uplifting message, some loving thoughts, and healing prayers.

Ten days later, Christine telephoned me to tell me, in her own words,

"You have given me the best ten days, I have had with my breathing for a long time now. In fact, in years."

I found it hard to believe, but again I asked myself why? Maybe it was my natural insecurities, which led me to believe otherwise. Was I lacking faith? I asked myself, yet again.

This dimension to God's work had me 'suspended 'in awe as much. I came to terms and began to embrace everything that has been 'given' and 'shown for it only transcends on the 'vibration' of love, and an understanding that 'anything', is possible'. when you believe.

It is only our 'psychical side' to our nature that limits us.

It is one of the same and comes from the same source, which encompasses God's Universal ' energy' of love, the highest and most powerful Spirit.

It was after that and during the years that followed I would have the occasional request of this type. I eventually rid myself of my insecurities about healing. I continued to oblige each time, resulting in a number of very positive responses.

Close friends and family would often ask me to lay my healing hands on them, for their occasional aches pains and injuries. Some people became converted and convinced by the healing power, as good results were founded.

I knew it was not only my faith but theirs also, that played an important part in the process of healing too. It helps when both participants have strong faith. That 'blind' faith I often speak about.

To embrace 'blind' faith, we must learn to also succumb to what appears to be God's will, which sometimes is the hardest lesson and a struggle for us all. All results stem from God's good purpose and reason. Whether we were trying to get relief, cure or knowledge.

We are all channels and healers. We not only heal with our touch but our words, our listening, our actions and our thoughts but most of all with our 'Faith'.

I began to understand all of this, when I was asked to 'lay on hands' once again. The request came from a desperate Grandmother whose three year old Grandson Bailey, had been diagnosed and treated for a brain tumour. He had been in remission for some time but the condition had returned. I met Bailey's Grandmother after a demonstration of my Mediumship. She asked if I could give him healing. I explained my understanding of the process of healing in the greatest detail to her. There was no question of a doubt to respond to her desperate plea . I felt humbled to be asked and we made arrangements a few days later.

I was to meet Bailey and his parents at their home in Coventry. I thought about the physical difficulty I might have. Was this little boy going to welcome me or even allow me near him? Let alone place my hands on him.

I had prayed for him and his family, each day, before the morning we met.

That morning I began to feel my 'senses' becoming heightened as I drove onto the housing estate where the family lived. Strange, sensitive thoughts unrelated to my visit penetrated my mind. There was something about the land I was driving across, I felt there was something chemical or geographical oozing up into the atmosphere. I soon dismissed those thoughts but there was good reason for why they came, it was confirmed later. I sensed that there was more than one neighbour, in the location, that had the same condition as Bailey. Maybe local 'pollution' had been a contributory factor in the cause of his illness. Those thoughts also confirmed my minds openness, the readiness to 'receive'. I then sensed my 'Guides' presence.

I was given a very warm welcome by Bailey's young parents. They introduced me to Bailey, who was their only child.

He was told that I was a lady who had come to talk to him. My presence didn't seem to bother him at all. He was more engrossed by the computer laptop that was on his knee. I was amazed at Bailey's computer skills for someone so young, and so ill. We started to chat, making the computer a focus of our conversation, not forgetting to include his other favourite subject, his robotic toy figures. I showed him the little Angel figurine, I had bought him; I knew it didn't match up to his beloved robots, so he wasn't exactly impressed. It became a talking point though, as we continued to chat. I was trying to 'connect' to his little soul.

It felt natural to just stroke his hair as we spoke. His father seemed very surprised that he allowed me to do that, as Bailey, was having difficulty allowing medical staff, let alone any stranger, near him. It was clear I had made a connection.

By sitting and chatting with Bailey I soon realised what an 'old soul' he was. He was way beyond his years, psychically and spiritually. It didn't surprise me when his parents told me of the 'adult' concern he showed and expressed to other children, as he'd met many along his little journey in the hospital wards and being part of a fund-raising campaign fronted by his parents. He had touched many a heart he'd met and a lot of little souls too.

There was certainly a presence about him, a wonderful aura. His character and personality shone, he didn't fail to 'touch' anyone. I sat with him for an hour or more, just stroking his hair and chatting. I was amazed by his mighty little spirit. He certainly touched my soul.

I also had the chance to talk in depth to Bailey's parents in intervals, they seemed fascinated by my work. It seemed that both parents were not of any particular religion as such. They opened up and shared their heart-breaking story of Bailey's struggles and triumphs, they seemed to grasp a new understanding of my beliefs and my spirituality, Bailey's mother more so, it seemed.

It came time to leave, we said our goodbyes, but before I could shut the door behind me Bailey's little voice shouted, "I like you... you can come and see me again." I was touched, just so humbled to of made that 'connection' with him.

Sadly it was the last time I would see and hear his physical presence.

I received an email some weeks later from Bailey's Grandfather explaining that Bailey had recently passed over very peacefully and that he wished to thank me for all the help and understanding that I had given his daughter in particular.

I was saddened by the news. I felt I didn't deserve any gratification what so ever, for it was the least I could have done. I examined the whole experience time and time again. It made me realize exactly what I had been a 'witness' to. Maybe not a direct healing but a healing' influence' had had been present in the room with the combination of Bailey's 'own soul's influence. After all I had no doubt I had been sitting in the presence of a' highly evolved' soul, one of purity, love and wisdom, a true 'Angel' whose journey on this earth plane, was destined to be short but very powerful. The impact he made through the power of his spirit and love left a major 'footprint., His purpose was to touch, and enact change to family, friends and all people for the better, on his ' life's short pathway to heaven once again.

His life, his love and his memory continues to make ripples as his spirit and his memory lives on helping children through charitable fund-raisers in his name.

I attended Bailey's funeral. It was such a sad but beautiful sight, a wonderful 'expression' of love. There was a white carriage, white horses, and fleet of white doves were included. So fitting for such a high soul., Above all the tears and sadness, it was a beautiful 'celebration' of his life here.

Bailey had transcended peacefully back to his heavenly 'home'…..

The Spiritual realms leaving a legacy of beneficial change behind him.

I gave service that week in a Church and was 'inspired' to tell the congregation a story ,all about ' The Day I met an Angel'. It ended with the influence of Bailey's spirit whose presence I felt, moments after I had finished the service, as this was confirmed by someone's 'mistake' as 'unknowingly' they played Bailey's funeral song.

Bailey had been a 'Gift' from God.

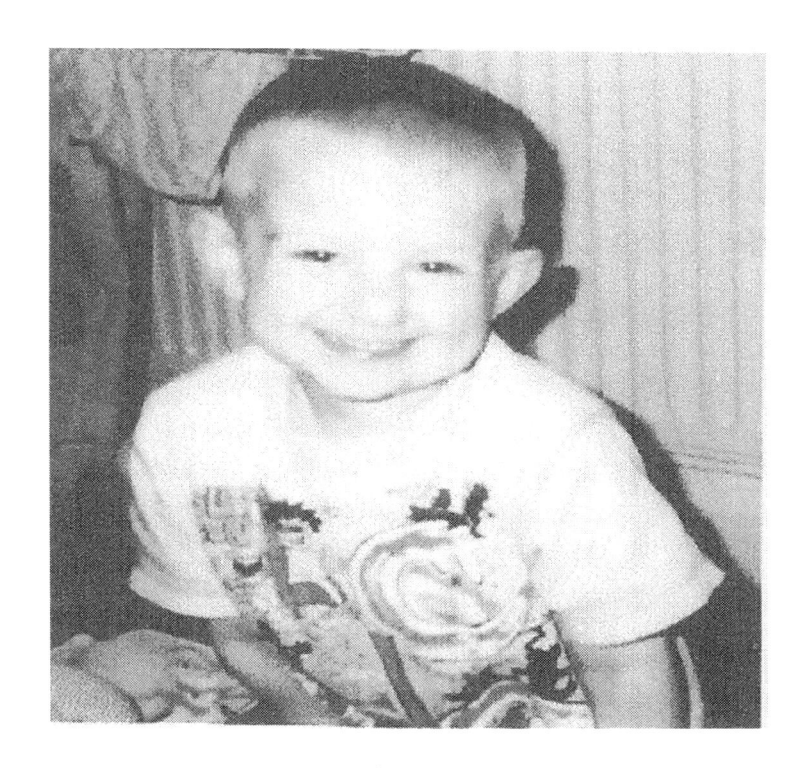

Bailey Wootten

Bless you my little 'Angel' friend and may your memory and spirit continue to bless people and all those who read this.

If you want to know a very simple way to connect to the right spirit, my advice is just pray. It is the true and only way to connect to Spirit. It is through meditative prayer.

Pray to God, God will show the way and give you things you can relate to. Pray to your Angels, and then to your loved ones, and preferably in that order.

When you do this, the understanding of the Hierarchy of the Spiritual Realms will fall into place. God is one of love, light and compassion. Regardless of your religion, remember that., ' All roads lead to that one God'.

I recall repeating this very statement once before when I was given a grand platform on a television programme. It was another opportunity to express my beliefs. It was the Sunday 'Religious and Ethical' debate programme called *The Big Question* hosted by Nicky Campbell. The debate subject issue was *Can we talk to Spirits and should we?* There were several Heads of Churches from a number of different denominations in the line-up. I was invited on as a Medium and Author to give my opinion on the subject. I gave as much explanation as I could in the short amount of time that I was allowed on camera.

It was at the end of the programme when Nicky Campbell was making a summary that something unexpected took place. It was almost like having a 'knee jerk reaction' a push from spirit. I found myself actually interrupting the' staged' order of the programme.

(I was being totally instrumented of course) and I then gave Nicky an impromptu reply, without any cue.. It shocked me as much him I think. I found myself gesturing to the front line- up of speakers, whilst looking at all the Heads of Churches present….. As I boldly said,

"When are we ALL going to realise that ALL roads lead to

that 'ONE GOD'!

It was one of very few statements that day that gave way to rapturous applause, and justifiably so too.

There are many 'gifts' that are given. There are those who seem to be born with a 'gift' of having an 'open' channel. That gift may come from the 'learning' they've had to endure from a previous life. I am a great believer in reincarnation as I have been a witness to too many experiences that have brought many inexplicable answers.

We only have to listen and observe young children in their play, as their meek, sensitive natures absorb and react like 'sponges' soaking up the energies from the Spiritual Realms. Children will often give us evidence of a previous life existence and the existence of an Afterlife too.

So take very special care of them as they are souls that have come before us and have arrived with a universal knowledge and they are same souls that are sent to set changes to our pathways for the better. They have come to share our journey, to teach us and touch our souls. It may be for the shortest of time but the love they leave behind is immeasurable. They leave 'foot prints' in our hearts which leads us to be in union once again. There are many 'Gifts' that are given and many to be discovered.

I believe in 'Miracles big and small' they are 'Gifts' too. We only have to 'seek' and we will 'find.' For those souls that 'seek' are those souls that have already been 'found'.

In the interim we seek answers from God and the Spiritual Realms, but above all, it is the love ,healing and comfort we gain that is paramount to our' spiritual wellbeing'. As in the words of my Spirit Guide:

'True Mediumship gives Flame to a Flickering Soul'

"I'm a little pencil in the hand of a writing God, who is sending a love letter to the world."

Mother Teresa

10 Typical Signs Of AUTISM

A.n.g.e.l — Autism Awareness Charity

Autism News Generating Education & Love

1. Not Responding To His/Her Name
2. Reacts To The Way Things Taste, Smell, Sound, Look And Feel
3. Having Poor Eye Contact, Prefers To Be Alone
4. Lack Of Response To Directions And Giving Unrelated Answers
5. Rarely Trying To Talk To Others
6. Gets Upset To Minor Changes
7. Language Delays
8. Doing Something Over And Over In Repetitive Play
9. Unusual Movements Like Flapping Hands Or Turning Hands In Circles
10. Rarely Smiling Back At Someone Who Smiles At Them

1 in 88 Children have Autism. With his smile and pure heart his family think he's 1 in a million

National Autistic Society
Helpline: 0808 800 4104
www.autism.org.uk

Autistic Society
www.autisticsociety.org

Advisory Centre for Education
Helpline: 0808 800 5793
www.ace-ed.org.uk

Contact a Family
Helpline: 0808 808 3555
www.cafamily.org.uk
www.cafamily.org.uk/Directa84.html

Ambitious About Autism
Tel: 020 8815 5444
www.ambitiousaboutautism.org.uk

IPSEA
Helpline: 0800 018 4016
www.ipsea.org.uk

UK Autism Awareness
www.autism-awareness.org.uk

Young Minds Parents Information Service
Helpline: 0808 802 5544
www.youngminds.org.uk

Autism Awareness Charity Non-Profit Organisation

Co.founder & Trustee A Meghee | Trustee J McCarthy | Trustee M Cope

Printed in Great Britain
by Amazon